PRAISE FOR *PROFESSIONAL TROUBLEMAKER*

"As an oft-scared chickenhead who cares too much about what others think, it's so comforting to be guided through my own crippling fear and self-doubt by one of the bravest, most incisively honest, hysterical voices I know. This book was so real and relatable, and so much of it had me belly laughing. This is the essential manual for anybody who is ready to take that leap of faith to bet on the best, uninhibited, whole version of themselves."

—**Issa Rae, actor, producer, creator of *Insecure*, and *New York Times* bestselling author**

"This book is a manual on HOW TO HUMAN. You could spend a lifetime and fortune finding the perfect therapist, mentor, minister, career coach, and girlfriend—or you could just spend a day reading *Professional Troublemaker*. This book—Luvvie Ajayi Jones's most helpful, bold, vulnerable, hilarious, and relevant work yet—is equal parts catharsis and wake-up call, both comforting and galvanizing. I laughed and cried so hard that my family asked me to read in the other room. With her razor-sharp mind, soul on fire, and heart of gold, Luvvie is the writer and artist the world needs right now. This will be my go-to gift for all the beloved trouble-makers in my life."

—**Glennon Doyle, author of the #1 *New York Times* bestseller *Untamed* and founder of Together Rising**

"There's nobody quite like Luvvie Ajayi Jones. She's a force and a powerhouse, the thunder and the lightning—and *Professional Troublemaker* shows us exactly how she got that way. This is a great book about reaching deep down inside yourself, crushing your fears, unleashing your 'too muchness,' and giving yourself permission to shake the world. In a voice that is funny, wise, bold, and always generous, Luvvie encourages, inspires, and dares us to follow our dreams, fight against injustice, soak up the pleasures of life, and take up all the space in the room. If this book doesn't make you feel bolder and braver by the final page, then you weren't reading it right. I loved every passionate word of it."

—**Elizabeth Gilbert, *New York Times* bestselling author of *Big Magic* and *Eat, Pray, Love***

"Whether you are traversing new territory, bounding back from perceived failure, or learning for the first time how to own the full power of your own voice, Luvvie's Fear-Fighting Manual is the pep talk we all need. Delivered in her singular voice and signature shade, this must-read is chock-full of gems that will guide you out of your own way so you can get more out of your life—a life that is more interesting than one lived in fear."

—**Elaine Welteroth, journalist and** *New York Times*
bestselling author of *More Than Enough*

"This book is a comfort and a challenge. It inspires, encourages, heartens, and invigorates in equal measure. You should read it."

—**Jenny Lawson,** *New York Times* **bestselling author of**
Furiously Happy **and** *Let's Pretend This Never Happened*

RISING
TROUBLEMAKER

RISING
TROUBLEMAKER

A Fear-Fighter Manual for Teens

LUVVIE AJAYI JONES

PHILOMEL

Philomel Books

An imprint of Penguin Random House LLC, New York

First published in the United States of America by Philomel Books,
an imprint of Penguin Random House LLC, 2022
This work is based on *Professional Troublemaker: The Fear-Fighter Manual* by Luvvie Ajayi
Jones, copyright © 2021 by Awe Luv, LLC, published by Penguin Life, an imprint of
Penguin Random House LLC

Copyright © 2021, 2022 by Awe Luv, LLC

Philomel Books is a registered trademark of Penguin Random House LLC.

Visit us online at penguinrandomhouse.com.

Library of Congress Cataloging-in-Publication Data is available.

Manufactured in Canada

ISBN 9780593526033

1   3   5   7   9   10   8   6   4   2

FRI

Edited by Jill Santopolo
Design by Lucia Bernard
Text set in Adobe Garamond Pro

I dedicate this book to my nieces and nephews,
Dejah, Destiny, Tooni, Obafemi, Darius, Kami, David.
I hope you all move through this world with courage,
knowing that you deserve everything good.

Contents

Introduction:
Make Good Trouble

<hr>

I am a professional troublemaker. And if you're reading this, I hope you are a RISING professional troublemaker, or you will become one.

What is a professional troublemaker, you ask?

A professional troublemaker is not the person who brings chaos into any room they are in. That person is a troll. A professional troublemaker is not someone who speaks just to hurt someone else's feelings. That person is a hater. A professional troublemaker is not someone who wants to disagree with people just because they wanna play devil's advocate. That person is a contrarian, and Satan never told anyone he needed a supervisor, so I'm not sure why so many people volunteer for the position.

A professional troublemaker is someone who knows this world

can be better than it currently is and is committed to being a part of the positive change. They're the person who is constantly wondering why people refuse to do better. They are the person who is themselves, without apology. As a writer, a speaker, and a shady Nigerian, I am the person who is giving the side-eye to folks for doing trash things. I am the person who can't keep quiet when I feel cheated. I am the person who says what folks are thinking and feeling but dare not say because they're afraid of how people will take it. My first book is even called *I'm Judging You: The Do-Better Manual*.

While a professional troublemaker isn't someone who creates chaos or crises, they do understand that chaos can come from being honest and authentic and going against the tide. Because in a world that insists on our cooperation even in the face of constant turmoil, not standing for it makes you a rebel. Professional troublemakers deal with it because they have a reason that is dear to their hearts. They are often sharp-tongued and misunderstood but always golden-hearted. A professional troublemaker is committed to speaking the truth and showing up always as themselves, and being proud of who they are, even as the world tells them they shouldn't be. To be a troublemaker is to be a disruptor working for the greater good. It's to be a changemaker. I think about the late, great congressman John Lewis, who challenged us with "Never, ever be afraid to make some noise and get in good trouble, necessary trouble." We must take up those arms.

People often ask me how I am confident in who I am, and how I have the nerve to say what I say. I've always shrugged and said I don't remember not being this person. Whenever I got in trouble when I was little, it was usually for my mouth. Being a Nigerian gal, I come from a culture that prioritizes age when it comes to giving respect, but that never sat well with me. That is why Little Luvvie got punished, usually for telling someone older that she didn't like what they were saying or doing.

But it's also because I come from a long line of professional troublemakers. My grandmother Olúfúnmiláyọ̀ Fáloyin* was the one I got to see as I was growing up. When I really give it thought, I realize I got a generation's worth of courage from Grandma.

My grandma was the chairlady of the board of directors of Team No Chill Enterprises. As an elder Nigerian stateswoman, she was the epitome of Giver of No Dambs.† She was too old to be checked. She knew how to take up the space she was given, and the times she wasn't given space, she took it. She did all of this with a smile and charm that made her magnetic. She wasn't rude, but she was direct. She wasn't hateful, but you would hear her speak her mind. She was openhearted and openhanded and she prayed with the same intensity that she'd use to scold you. She could not stand to see people cheated or treated poorly. Given her honesty and the

---

*Pronounced Oh-LOO-foon-me-LAH-yaw FAH-low-YEEN.
†Damb: Because it's more fun than "damn." Get used to this.

fact that she approached everything with so much heart, she was deeply loved by so many.

This is the core of what it means to be a professional troublemaker. She is who I watched, and who told me I could be that and still be loved.

WHEN TROUBLEMAKING MEETS FEAR

My first book, *I'm Judging You: The Do-Better Manual*, asks us all to commit to leaving this world better than we found it. I wrote *Professional Troublemaker: The Fear-Fighter Manual* and *Rising Troublemaker* because in order to do better and live your truly best life, you gotta do some scary things. This book is the HOW to *I'm Judging You*'s WHAT. In *Rising Troublemaker*, I want to tell you the things I wish adults had told me growing up. I want to pass on the lessons I've learned (sometimes painfully) so I can shield you from some of the trash of the world.

There is a lot to be afraid of in this world. There is a lot to navigate. To be a troublemaker is to commit to facing our fears over and over again.

In November 2017, I opened the TEDWomen conference with a talk called "Get Comfortable with Being Uncomfortable," which addressed this very subject. When the talk was posted online, it was watched more than one million times in a month. At this point, it has received over seven million views and continues to climb. Every single day, I get messages from people from all over the world talking about how much impact it had on them, and that lets me know that this idea of living through fear is something that a lot of us struggle with. We are afraid of simply showing up in the world, and it affects everything around us as a result.

But here's the thing: We're human. Fear is God's way of making sure we're not being utterly stupid and jumping off mountains without parachutes. God is like, "Let me put something in these beings I'm creating so they aren't constantly coming back here before their time. Because I know they need limits." However, the same tool that keeps us from putting our hand in an open fire and leaving it there is the same one keeping us from telling our friends that they've hurt our feelings because of something they said.

One of the things I've learned is how much fear could have stopped me, at any moment, from doing the thing that changed my life. Or doing the thing that led to me meeting the right person. Or doing the thing that allowed someone else to do the thing that changed their life. We talk about "living our best lives," but how are we gonna do it when we have fear holding our ankles down like some dad sneakers? (I will never understand why them bulky dad sneakers are a thing. Your feet look like they're embedded in some rocks as you drag those things around all day. Why are people against nice things? Anyway, I digress.)

I don't think we can overcome fear. It's a constant fight, and we will get endless opportunities to do scary shit. I'm not going to sit up here and say, "This is how I get rid of fear." We will always be afraid of something. What we need to do is stop expecting fearlessness and acknowledge that we're anxious but we aren't letting fear be our deciding factor. I think to be "FEARLESS" is to not allow FEAR to make you do LESS.

Folks like me, the professional troublemakers who are committed to speaking truth to power, aren't doing it without fear. We aren't doing it because we are unafraid of consequences or sacrifices we are making because of it. We are doing it because we have to. We know we must charge forward regardless. We must listen to the wisdom of mother Maya Angelou when she said, "Courage is the most important of all the virtues, because without courage you can't practice any other virtue consistently. You can practice any virtue erratically, but nothing consistently without courage."

For the professional troublemaker, the truth—of ourselves and of the things around us—is more important than the fear that stops us from pursuing it. The things we must do are more powerful than the things we are afraid to do. Professional troublemakers recognize that fear is real, and that it's an everlasting hater, but it must be tackled.

This book is a middle finger up to fear.

Now, I say all this acknowledging that there are systems that make saying "Fight fear" riskier for some of us. Our marginalized identities compound the risk of wanting to step out of and over our comfort zones. I know that it can be a privilege to be in the position where you feel like you have the choice to be a professional troublemaker. That is why I'm hoping that this book, written by a Black woman, an immigrant who was poor at some point (but didn't know it), somehow allows you to have the gumption to be a troublemaker for yourself.

I think it is important that we know what our problems are, and that we create the solutions for them. We need to create the world we prefer to live in.

That being said, everything I ask of you in this book I ask of myself first, and I ask of myself always. This book is my excuse to tell *ME* to continue to make trouble in the best ways. It is me giving myself permission to not be fearless, because fearlessness doesn't exist. I think the fear will always be there, but what's important is that I go forward anyway. This isn't a life of sine metu (Latin for "without fear"). It is a life of "I might be afraid, but I won't let it stop me."

What I'm sharing in this book is what I would have loved to tell thirteen-year-old me so that she could always find the confidence to be different. Along with: Don't let them glue that weave in your hair for that college dorm fashion show. It's gonna pull out your hair and sabotage your edges for a couple months. It ain't worth it.

This is also the book I needed when:

- I knew I really didn't want to become a doctor, but since it was the dream I'd tied myself to since I was little, I was afraid of choosing something else.

- I didn't call myself a writer even though I'd been writing four times a week for nine years, and my words were reaching people in ways I'd never imagined.

- I was asked to give the biggest talk of my career and I turned it down two times before saying yes because I didn't think I was ready, and I was afraid I'd bomb onstage.

This is also a book I need now, in the times when I'm not feeling so bold. It's a book from me to me that I'm letting other people read. Because even now, I still need the prompts I've put here. Even now, I still need to remind myself to do the scary shit I'm compelled to do and deal with how it falls. Even now, I still stop myself from time to time. This book is for me: the me from yesterday, the me from today, and the me in the future who will need the extra push. It is the book I want to give to my kids one day to embolden them to move through this world unburdened.

In the BE section, I'll be talking about the things we must get right within us before we can do the things that scare us. Because half the battle is with our own selves and our own insecurities. We gotta Harlem Shake it off. (Did I just age myself? I'm fine with it.)

In the SAY section, I'll be pushing us to use our voices for our own greater good, and therefore everyone else's. We're so afraid to say the things that are necessary, and it is part of the reason why we find ourselves constantly fighting a world that doesn't honor us. We've gotta say what is difficult even when our voices shake.

In the DO section, I'll be encouraging us to start putting movement to that voice we're unsilencing. A Ralph Waldo Emerson quote I love is "What you do speaks so loudly that I cannot hear what you say." It is time for our actions to start proving the truth of our words.

Throughout this book, I'm also going to share stories of my grandmother, because her life is truly my biggest lesson on living beyond your fears.

My hope is that the next time you want to do something that takes your breath away as you think about it, you'll find words in this book that tell you, "Yo. You got this. Even if it fails, you will be okay."

So . . . let's get to it.

BE

We have to make some internal shifts if we wanna fight fear, because what we think is possible is a major part of how far we can go. In the BE section, we're going to talk through the work we gotta do within us so that even when we're afraid, we move forward anyway.

"TO KNOW OURSELVES IS TO WRITE OUR VALUES IN CEMENT EVEN IF OUR GOALS ARE IN SAND."

—Luvvie Ajayi Jones

1

KNOW YOURSELF

We fear our full selves.

 We are afraid of who we are, in all our glory (and grit). We're constantly searching for that person. Or forgetting that person. Or repressing that person. Instead of standing strong in who that person is.

Being FULLY ourselves, without apology or shame, serves as a grounding force in a shaky world. There are a lot of things to be afraid of, but one of those things should not be YOU, in all your amazingness.

Standing in your full self does not mean you are unyielding and super stubborn and can't nobody tell you nothing. It does not mean you're not able to admit when you're wrong. Instead, it's about having a strong sense of identity. It's about knowing you belong in this world just as much as anyone else. It's about taking up the space you earned simply by being born.

One of my favorite poems is "Desiderata," written by Max Ehrmann. My favorite part is "You are a child of the universe / no less than the trees and the stars; you have a right to be here . . ."

"YOU HAVE A RIGHT TO BE HERE." You sure do.

Knowing this fullness of who you are doesn't make you more stubborn. Instead, it makes you more likely to grow, since you know you have a solid foundation that doesn't change even as you learn new things and new perspectives. This is a step you need to take to be a professional troublemaker. Because you will GET IN TROUBLE. Guaranteed. What makes you realize it's worth it? Knowing that you are enough, you are valuable, and you are loved, for simply being you.

A lot of fear fighting and professional troublemaking is confronting things that might shake us up. Things that might slap us into dizziness and make us forget everything we know is real. We need solid feet, rooted in something strong, to continue to stand. Knowing ourselves is important because it provides that foundation for us. It doesn't allow anyone or anything to tell us who we are. Because when people tell us how amazing we are, that's good to absorb. But what about when someone tells us we aren't worthy? Or we don't have value? Or we don't deserve kindness and love? Or we deserve paper cuts? To know thyself is to not take all the praise to head or take all the shaming to heart. To know ourselves is to write our values in cement even if our goals are in sand.

To know thyself is to know your core, and for me, to know my core is to feel rooted in something outside myself. It is to know not only *who* I am but *whose* I am.

WHOSE WE ARE

Whose I am is not about belonging to someone or being beholden to people. It is about the community you are tied to that holds you accountable. It is about knowing you are part of a tribe that is greater than yourself. It is about feeling deeply connected to someone and knowing that no matter where you go, home is always waiting for you. If we're phones, knowing whose we are is our charging station (or cord).

I learned the importance of WHOSE you are growing up. As a Yorùbá girl, I am part of a tribe that prioritizes its people sometimes as much as it prioritizes an individual. Collectivism comes alive for us through the traditional oríkì (OH-ree-kee).

What's an oríkì? It's a Yorùbá word that combines two words to mean "praising your head/mind." *Orí* is "head" and *kì* is "to greet or praise." An oríkì is a greeting that praises you through praising your kinship and speaking life to your destiny. It is your personal hype mantra and can be spoken or sung.

The original attempts to tell you who you are make up your oríkì. It's used to remind you of your roots and your history. It might include the city your father's from, and where his father is from. It might include the things that make your family name special. It brags on your people. It lets people know who you WERE, who you ARE, and who you WILL BE. It reminds you of those who came before you and blesses those who will come after. It might even include some shade.

Oríkìs are often sung at birthdays and celebrations. They are also sung to see you off into the next life. An oríkì connects you to your ancestors, and it will move even the most stoic to cry because you feel it in your chest. Your tear ducts just give up the ghost and let the water go.

I am the granddaughter of a woman named Olúfúnmiláyọ̀ Juliana Fáloyin, and she's the one who serves as my compass. When Grandma would say her own name, she'd always say it with a smile. Which makes sense, because her name literally means "God gave me joy." It was like her very self and presence brought her joy. When they sang my grandmother's oríkì at her funeral, I got emotional because it was a poetic affirmation of her presence on this earth and a send-off. It was a standing ovation for her spirit.

This is part of my grandma's oríkì:

Ọmọ Ògbóni Modù lorè, mẹ̀rẹ̀ ní àkún
Ọmọ Fulani Ìjẹ̀sà a múni má parò oko ọni
Ọmọ a fi ọsẹ fọsọ kí ómọ Ẹlòmíràn fi eérú fọ ti ẹ̀
Ọmọ arúgbìnrin owó bọ̀dìdẹ̀
Ọmọ Olúmoṣe atìkùn àyà fọhùn
Ògbóni gbà mí, Ọ̀dọ̀fin gbà mí
Ẹ níí tó níí gbà lẹ̀ gbani

What it loosely means (because there are some Yorùbá words
that don't exist in English, and it is really tough to give exact
meaning) is:

The child of royalty . . .
The child of the Ìjẹ̀sà Fulani who dominates one and
    dominates one's property
The child who brings out soap to wash their own
    clothes while someone else's child brings out ashes
    to wash theirs
The child that springs up money (wealth) in
    multiples
The child who beats their chest as they speak (speak
    with confidence)

Ògbóni, save me, Ọdọfin, save me

It is the one that is prominent enough to save you that
     steps up to do it

Her oriki ties her back to those who came before her and gasses
her up. I don't know my oríkì. Many of us don't. Like a lot of
traditions, oríkìs have been deprioritized as generations pass. I'm
out here oríkì-less AF. But it's okay. I'm fine, really. I'm not mad at
all that by the time I came along, folks were more blasé about
it (clearly I'm low-key salty, but I'll deal with that with my therapist).

However, a lot of what we already do is derivative of oríkìs and
we don't even realize it. The tradition of the oríkì isn't just in
Yorùbáland; it's gone on through the diaspora. You can see it in the
way people rap about themselves. It's in the way people praise God.
It's in the way we say who we are in the moments we feel most
proud.

When Christians praise God, we say: King of kings. Lord of
lords. Alpha and Omega. The Beginning and the End. The I am.
The Waymaker. That's an oríkì if I ever heard one.

You might be too young to have watched the TV show *Game
of Thrones* when it first came out, but in it, there is a character
named Daenerys Targaryen. Whenever she walked into a room,
she got this HYPE introduction: "Daenerys Stormborn of the
House Targaryen. First of Her Name. The Unburnt. Queen of the

Andals and the First Men. Khaleesi of the Great Grass Sea. Breaker of Chains. Mother of Dragons." THAT IS SUCH AN ORÍKÌ! Don't you feel gassed up on her behalf? I know I do. That's what it is for!

I tend to write oríkìs for people I admire to gas them up as I please. I've done a few in the past.

For Michelle Obama: Michelle LaVaughn of House Obama. First of Her Name. Dame of Dignity. Melanin Magnificence. Chic Chicagoan. Boss Lady of Brilliance. Owner of the Arms of Your Envy. Forever First Lady.

For Beyoncé: Beyoncé Giselle of House Carter. First of Her Name. Snatcher of Edges. Killer of Stages. Citizen of Creole Wonderland. Legendary Black Girl. Wakandan Council President.

For Oprah: Oprah Gail of House Winfrey. First of Her Name. Changer of the World. Protector of the Realm of Noirpublic. Creator of Paths. Breaker of Chains and Limits.

For Janelle Monáe: Janelle of House Monáe. First of Her Name. Citizen of the Future. Walker of Tightropes. Rocker of the Baddest Suits. Head Android of Wondaland.

For Simone Biles: Simone Arianne of House Biles. First of Her Name. Aerial Assassin. Code of Points Champion. Somersault Sorceress. Flipping Fanatic. Mocker of Gravity. Duchess of Dismounts. Obliterator of the Olympic Order.

For Amanda Gorman: Amanda of House Gorman. First of Her Name. Prophetess of Prose. Anointed Artist. Dignified Dreamer. Sage Scribe. Highborn Verse Slayer. Noble of Noir Pixie Dust®.

For Yara Shahidi: Yara of House Shahidi. First of Her Name. Builder of Generational Bridges. Teller of Truths. Thoughtful Activist. "It" Factor Maven. Brilliant Being. Niece Goals. Taker of Fierce Photos.

So, I want you to have one of your own. How do you write a *Game of Thrones*–style oríkì for yourself? Here's the formula:

First Name and Middle Name of House Last Name. Number of Her/His/Their Name (e.g., Juniors are "Second of Their Name").

That's the easy part.
The next part: Throw humility away. The point of this is to

give yourself ALL the credit. I want you to acknowledge the things that make you proud and the things you have accomplished. They can be things that you are known for. They don't have to just be about an award, but they can be things that feel like your superpower. Feel free to use noble titles for yourself (Queen, King, Earl, Duchess), because why not? Get creative with your descriptors if you want. I am also a fan of throwing some alliteration in there for extra pizzazz.

Noun (occupation or descriptor) of Noun (thing).

Here's mine:

Luvvie of House Jones. First of Her Name. Assassin of the Alphabet. Bestseller of Books. Conqueror of Copy. Dame of Diction. Critic of Culture. Sorceress of Side-Eyes. Eater of Jollof Rice. Rocker of Fierce Shoes. Queen of the Jones Kingdom. Taker of Stages. Nigerian Noble and Chi-Town Creator.

I could keep going, but I'll stop here. You need one of your own, and I want you to write it. Now, if you have the time. If not, come back to it. Or you can get with your friends and y'all can create yours together.

I know you might be thinking, *But those people Luvvie mentioned are famous and extraordinary and hugely dope. I can't even measure up to that.* And to that, I say, "NOPE NOPE NOPE." I want you to leave that kinda talk behind. Because yes, those are some incredibly visible people, and they have achieved a lot.

But so have you. By being here on this earth, you have done enough, and you have SO MUCH life left to live to get some cool professional titles. (We'll deal with impostor syndrome in a few chapters.) A lot of those people are older than you. What the future holds for you will be amazing!

Besides, you can be Giver of Best Hugs, Fortnite Champion, TikTok Titan, Ravishing Reader, Debonair Dancer . . . there are so many things about you that are worthy of praise, so put them on paper and don't be shy about bragging on yourself!

What if you have a complicated relationship with your family? Or you were adopted, so you don't know your biological family history? For those who might not have blood ties to the people they love most, you are still part of a people who cherish you, adore you, and are glad that you are here on this earth in this space and time. To you, I send love. Not knowing the binds that tie you by blood does not exclude you from belonging to a people or a community or a tribe.

If you are someone who can truly say you don't have an answer to WHOSE you are, and this book has made it to you and these words are being heard or read by you, then you are truly someone who should laugh at fear. Cackle at it, even. Having no one is not a cause for shame here but one for pride, because it means you have moved through the world, drop-kicking these obstacles by yourself. You are a warrior. Your oríkì can start with ARMY OF ONE. You have battled so many challenges by yourself, and you are still standing and finding reasons to smile every day! You are still here, and I am really proud of you! High-five yourself. Army of One. Solo Soldier. Fierce Warrior. Rock of Gibraltar has nothing on you.

Everybody needs an oríkì.

I need you to spend this time bragging on yourself. Type this up, write it up, put it somewhere you will remember. Laminate it, even. You will need this one day—in the moments when you see the worst of yourself or you fall flat on your face. You will need this when you feel like you have failed or when someone tries to make you feel bad about yourself. Or when you don't get that scholarship or internship you really wanted. Or when you fall out with a close friend. You will need this.

You know those times when you're talking and between every word, you're clapping your disbelief because someone talked to you like you're small? Yeah, those too. In those times, you can read your oríkì and remind yourself who you be (yes, who you be). I want you to have this thing handy, to bring you back to the reality of how dope you are.

Cool? Cool.

WHO WE ARE

Beyond knowing WHOSE we are, there's knowing WHO we are. Outside of our connections to anyone else, we have to know what is important. I know that all too often, we won't say what we want or need, and then we'll sit in frustration. We might lose the appetite to be ourselves because it's been insulted, beaten, bullied, punished, abused, and made fun of out of us. We look up one day and realize we've let the world, or our classmates, or our disciplinarians, convince us that we are not good enough. It's tough!

It is no fault of our own. And it is by design that we try really hard to fit in. I am always taken aback when people ask me how I am so confident. I am confident because I am constantly doing work to ensure that I do not lose sight of me, so I never have to go looking for me. When we are sure-footed in who we are, we always have something to come back to. When we know what defines us is not how great our grades are or what sports we play, we are less likely to lose our way if we lose any of those accomplishments.

Let me double down on that. You deserve to be loved, defended, and affirmed, no matter what grades you get, how you score on exams, or what titles you win. You matter, right here, right now, flawed and all. You matter. Do all you can to never forget that or lose sight of that.

We have bad days where we question our own worth. And when those days come, I look at my life's mission statement to reset me. What is that? Well, it is an exercise that has allowed me to put ME on paper. I ask myself the following questions, and then I write the answers down. My fairy godmentor (she doesn't know I've claimed her as that), Oprah, often talks about what we know to be true. Well, these questions have given me clarity to figure that out.

What do you hold dear?

This is what is important to you. Is it family? Is it friends? Is it your well-curated Spotify playlist that you and your friends have worked on for the last three years? Who (or what) do you cherish in your life?

What are your core values?

Our core values are what we stand for and what guide us. Mine are:

Honesty: This is one of my top values, partly because I'm a bad liar and have a terrible poker face. But mostly because I want to feel trusted by those who know me. It's important that I am one less person others need to doubt.

Authenticity: I am who I am, no matter where I am or who I'm with. Authenticity is close to the honesty core value because it insists that I be honest about myself and how I show up. It doesn't mean I am the same all the time, but it means if I'm quiet, it's because I am allowing myself to observe in the moment. If I'm partying and being the life of the party, in that time I am feeling boisterous.

Benevolence: I think it's important to be kind, and being generous with the things we have is a major part of that, whether it's knowledge or time or money or energy. It means we are less selfish about our lives and think about what we can constantly give to the collective for the greater good.

Shea butter: Yes, shea butter is a core value because I think we'd all be better if we were more moisturized. Get some good body butter in your life and watch your life change. You wake up without rustling your sheets with your extreme ash.

What brings you joy?

What makes your heart smile? Helping people by telling them what I know brings me joy. Having people tell me something I did or said made an impact on them melts my heart. Yes, there's a Captain Save-a-Planet complex there, but I'm working that out with my therapist.

Even on your worst day, what makes you amazing?

At a time when you aren't in the mood to be the best you, what still makes you incredible, just as you are?

What is worth fighting for, even if your arms are too short to box with God?

Let's say you know your uppercut is weak and your jab is rubbish. What will make you lace up your gloves anyway? What do you think you will make the "no violence" exception for? I know I can't fight worth a damb, so I gotta be clear on what will push me to fight if necessary. For me, it's seeing someone who doesn't deserve it be abused or rendered defenseless or voiceless.

What do you want them to say when they're lowering you into the ground?

When it is my time to leave this earth, I want people to say, "The world was better because she was here." I also wanna make sure whoever tries to act like they wanna jump in with me because they're auditioning for Best Mourner of the World, y'all tell them to sit their ass down because this ain't the time for them to be attention whores. I'll be giving them a fierce side-eye from beyond.

All of these questions are things I've asked and continue to ask myself, because when I've written the answers down and I go over them, they are the best memento of me. They are my life mission statement. They are my guide when I find myself off course after a tough day or week or season.

YOUR LIFE MISSION STATEMENT

Write your own life mission statement, your compass. Here's the template. Fill this out.

What's your name?

Who are you proud to be related to? Who are you proud to be friends with?

Even on your worst day, what makes you amazing?

What/who do you hold dear? What do you cherish?

What are your core values? What do they mean?

What brings you joy?

What is worth fighting for, even if your arms are too short to box with God?

What do you want them to say when they're lowering you into the ground?

Here is mine:

I am Ìfẹ́olúwa Luvvie Àjàyí Jones. I am the granddaughter of Fún-miláyọ̀ Fáloyin and the daughter of Yẹmisí Àjàyí.* I am the wife of Carnell Jones. Even on my worst day, I can look in the mirror and be proud of the woman I've become. I have no regrets. My family, both blood and chosen, are who I hold dear. What I cherish is my life, lived happy, whole, and healthy. My core values are honesty, authenticity, benevolence, and shea butter. This means I tell the truth, I'm real to myself and others, I'm generous, and I refuse to be ashy because I should always prioritize being moisturized.

 It brings me joy when I'm able to make someone else's life easier. Also, seeing my enemies upset. Because: petty. I didn't say Jesus was done working on me yet. What I fight for are people who feel like they are powerless or voiceless. When I'm no longer here, I want people to say, "The world was better because she was here."

---

*Yorùbá is a beautiful tonal language whose alphabet uses accents to reflect the sounds. You'll see those accents on the Yorùbá words I have used throughout this book. My name, my grandmother's name, and my mother's name are written here fully accented to honor the traditional language. Moving forward, the accents won't be present on my and my mom's names because we don't use these accents in our everyday lives.

Colloquially and in the world, Yorùbá words, especially names, are often written without accents. When I write my own name, I don't include the accents, and I wanna honor myself in that. I went back and forth about this decision of whether to include them in our names throughout the book, and then I asked my mom for her opinion. She said, "I don't think it's necessary. We are who we are, with or without the accents."

I honor tradition as I honor self.

You can show it to others, but you don't have to. Above all, it is for you to have.

This exercise not only lets you know who you are on paper, it also shows you who you aren't. We are often weighed down by other people's ideas of who they think we are. We are regularly defined by systems, stereotypes, and structures that are larger than us. To know who we are is to insist on knowing we are not what others put on us. We are not the names people call us. We are not our worst moments or mistakes. So when people try to put all this pain and trauma on us, we can say, "Nah. That's not my problem." Once you know who you are, it's easier to refute who you aren't.

Do you know who you are? Do you know how much fight it took for you to be wherever you are today? Do you know how many things could have gone wrong to keep you from even being born? Do you know that none of the people you are scared of and none of the situations you're afraid of are bigger than any of that? Do you understand how dope you are? You are here now, and one thousand dust buckets shouldn't be able to tell you anything that makes you feel like you don't deserve good things.

Don't let people who can't spell your name right tell you about who you are. Don't let folks who only have courage behind a keyboard define your goodness or your worth as a person. Do not let people whose parents still have to tell them to brush their teeth diminish your value. Do not let people who are already rooting for you to fall insist on your value, because they will steer you wrong.

When you are tempted to believe someone's wrong version of you, reread your mission statement. Remind yourself of how incredible you are before trying to remind anyone else. Because, ultimately, the world will continue to misunderstand us. We can't control that. What we can control is our own image of ourselves and how much we are worth caring for, loving, and defending. In all of our messed-up, scared glory.

Your professional troublemaking depends on it.

I hope you feel hyped up! I hope this is a chapter you are able to come back to time and time again. I hope in future chapters, when I ask you to do things that might be tough, you feel encouraged and know that you are okay. And that you are reminded that you are a legacy of a lot of things going right.

2

BE TOO MUCH

We fear being judged for being different.

 When we talk about people being their full selves and how a lot of folks are afraid of it, it's not that people don't want to show up as themselves. It's that they know that when they show up in their full splendor, they might be judged for it. Being ordinary and unremarkable is hardly a life goal, but we are often scared into being that way.

Even though people like to act fake-offended at the idea that they're being judged, we know good and well that we are all judging each other. We just happen to critique each other on the wrong things, like what we look like, who we love, what deity we worship, if any. Instead, we should assess each other on how kind we are, how we're showing up for other humans, and how we're contributing to the world's problems, large or small. (I also like to judge people on whether they drink kombucha, because I don't understand how anyone can appreciate something that tastes like moldy milk, toenail clippings, and bad decisions. But that's beside the point.)

We judge each other and are judged every single day on who we are and how we are. And oftentimes, people bang their internal gavel on us and decide that we are too much.

TOO (adverb): to an excessive extent or degree; beyond what is desirable, fitting, or right (Dictionary.com)

To be TOO something is to do or be something to a level that folks find to be uncouth or uncomfortable. It's to be different.

Many of us have been called too loud. Or too aggressive. Or too passionate. Or too intimidating. Or even too quiet. Or too sensitive. Or too tall. Or too short. Or too Black. Or too weird. And when people say we are TOO something, they aren't making a casual observation. They are requesting that we change this thing, that we turn the volume down. Then we feel self-conscious or embarrassed and turn inwardly to fix something about ourselves that someone else has defined as a problem.

The dilemma: what we've been told is too much is usually

something that is core to who we are, or how we appear, and often it's something we cannot change.

How is someone too tall? Should they hunch over to come down to your level? How is someone too Black? Should they peel their skin off their body to have less melanin? How is someone too weird? What's NORMAL, anyway? Unfortunately, we internalize these critiques, and it leads to us worrying about being different in any way.

I remember what it was like to be young, in school and doing my best to fit in. I definitely did all I could not to be "TOO" something, and it usually didn't work. No matter how hard I tried, I still stood out. What I wish I knew then that I know now is that I didn't have to be ashamed of my differences. And that one day, I'd look back on that time and go, "I'm glad you weren't like everyone else." Being hard to forget is really coming in handy right now, I'll tell you that much.

As a Black woman who is opinionated, straightforward, and unapologetic about it, I am secretary of Team Too Much. I even bring the kettle corn to our monthly meetings. I've been considered aggressive or loud or angry for simply being direct. Black girls and women are often on the receiving end of the "too loud," "too brash," "too aggressive" notions, because our very being has become synonymous with too much. I'm convinced it's because people see the divine in us and it is too bright for them to deal with. Meanwhile, they better put their shades on and deal with all this Noir Pixie Dust®.*

I especially resist "too aggressive." When someone says that, did they see us randomly walk up to someone on the street and punch them in the mouth? Did we push someone into a wall for no reason? Did we cuss a nun out? Or is it that we didn't put enough eager exclamation points or emojis in the emails we sent a classmate? Did we ask for what we wanted in straightforward terms? How are we being aggressive? What have we done to earn that title? At least let me earn whatever you accuse me of.

Being accused of TOO MUCHness is to be told to take up less space. Being TOO MUCH is to be excessive. How do you combat that? By being less than you are. And that concept feels like nothing other than self-betrayal. The opposite of too much is too little. I'd rather be too big than too small any day.

Can you imagine if someone walked up to you and said to your face, "I need you to be less"? You'd be offended. But THAT is what they're saying when they say you're too much—they're just saying it in a less accusing and more shaming manner, so you take it to heart. You personalize and absorb it and commit to changing yourself.

All for what? For the whims of people who are more fickle than

---

*Noir Pixie Dust® is what I consider to be the magic of Black people, especially Black women. Yes, I trademarked it. You know people like to steal from us.

a ripening avocado. (Seriously, how are avocados okay when you go to bed, and then you wake up to something that looks like a kiwi? Wonders shall never cease.)

Who we are should not be based on the moods of the people we are around, their insecurities, or their projections. Because when someone says you are too much, it is more of a statement on them than on you.

You ARE too tall for that short person. Your height makes their neck hurt, but what's that gotta do with you?

You ARE too aggressive for that complacent person. Your passion irritates their inactivity.

You ARE too quiet for that disruptive person. Your calm makes them agitated.

You ARE too Black for that white person. Your melanatedness is garish to their caucasity.

You ARE too big for that small space. Your vastness chokes its insignificance.

In all of these, your job is not to stop being this person you are accused of being. You aren't supposed to constantly shape-shift to make those around you feel better about their own insecurities or failures. Your job is not to chameleon your way through life to the point where you forget what your true colors are.

If you are too big, then it's a reflection that the place you're in is too small for you. It isn't your job to get smaller to fit there, but to find a place that is bigger than you so you can take up all the space you want and grow infinitely. Any place that demands you shrink is a place that will suffocate your spirit and leave you gasping for air. Who wins? Not you. Not anyone, really, because the version of you that they will get is the diet, fake-sugar, stevia version that probably has a bad aftertaste. They might THINK that's a great version because you're so dope that even you at half capacity is more on point than you expect. BUT they don't get the you who is free to show up and be your best, because you are spending time trying to be whatever they think is palatable. And that constant shrinking and dwindling is how giants get locked in cages. You don't belong in a cage simply because it's where others want you to be.

My grandmother was the Queen Mother of Team Too Much International Association of Extra People. Being too much was woven into her spirit. She was too bossy, too confident, too aggressive, too brash, too headstrong, too assertive, too feisty, too strong, too dramatic. Mama Fáloyin, as so many people called her, was the definition of boisterous. Everything she did was big, and I don't think it occurred to her to ever shrink herself.

Let's talk about her theatrics. As an older Nigerian woman, being too dramatic was destiny fulfillment. In fact, her entire existence demanded that after she got to a certain age, she had to be melodramatic; otherwise she wasn't doing it right. It made her a joy to be around even when she was upset, because it was often super amusing.

Grandma used to come to the United States once a year and stay with us for a couple of months at a time. She had a tendency to do the most, so of course she and my mom would clash from time to time. One day in particular, they had a major argument, and Grandma, in all her feistiness, got extra upset.

This lady suddenly went in her room, threw a few things in a trash bag, put on her shoes, and came into the living room. She had on her house scarf, socks, and sandals. She threw on her coat and grabbed her purse. She looked ridiculous cuz nothing matched or went together, but that was part of the act. We asked her where she was going, and she replied with "I'm leaving. I'm going to go sit at the bus stop and wait for the people who pick up old people to come and get me." I didn't know when the laugh escaped my mouth, but it was too late to catch it. I cackled! She looked at me, all serious, almost offended.

ME: Grandma, who will pick you up?

GRANDMA: I don't know. Someone will take pity on me and come get me.

I wanted to be like, "Lady, stahp it." But I couldn't because I was not about to be the target of her wrath, so I had to fake-beg her to stay. You know she wasn't going anywhere. The trash bag made no sense, because this woman had perfectly good luggage, but she had to do her one-woman show. Also, is there some sort of random old-people pickup service that I haven't heard about? Like a dog-catcher for elders? Like a free Uber service for hysterical geriatrics? Whew! It was hilarious. You might say it was too dramatic, but at least it was amusing.

And TOO EXTRA? Well, she was a pro at that. When my grandmother turned sixty years old in 1991, she decided to do a seven-day celebration to commemorate her life. It was in Ìbàdàn, Nigeria, where she lived and where I grew up. She rented three huge tents and closed off three blocks in front of and surrounding her house for the festivities. No one had to RSVP because everyone was invited. I don't think folks counted, but there had to be about a thousand people who came each day. The jollof rice was endless. Grandma hired Ebenezer Obey, who was Nigeria's top musician at the time, to come sing and perform from evening to sunup. Literally. He got off the stage at 6:00 a.m. She threw three major parties in those seven days, and her church choir performed. Come on, holy concert! They showed what an anointed turnup really is. We members of her family wore aṣọ ẹbí* the whole time. Mama Fálo-yin herself wore the heaviest of laces, and gold chains so big she'd make some rappers jealous. She had two cakes for each day. I especially remember the one that was in the shape of a Bible, because: super Christian. The whole celebration was A LOT. Some might even say it was too much. But why not? How many times do you turn sixty? Once! Do it big, ma'am!

Whether you thought my grandma was TOO anything, you didn't wanna miss that party. This same woman who people thought was too loud was the one people came to, to help them raise a ruckus when they were being treated unfairly or had a problem with some figure of authority. She was loud not only for herself but for people who she thought didn't have a voice to be loud for themselves. I remember plenty of times when we'd get visitors who were looking to her to mediate a conflict they were having with someone who was trying to cheat them. One phone call from her and it would be resolved. Her loudness was not just in service of herself, and people didn't consider her TOO loud when it was in their favor. It is also why she was deeply honored.

---

*Aṣọ ẹbí (pronounced ah-shaw eh-BEE) is Yorùbá for "clothes of kin." It's matching fabric we wear for special occasions, and it signifies to people that those in it are close family and friends of whoever is celebrating.

am a proud Nigerian woman. But when I was nine, I moved from Nigeria to the United States and started at a new school, and my confidence in myself was shaken for the first time ever. It was the first time in my life that I felt like I needed to shrink myself because I was too much. I was too different.

(Let the record also show that I didn't know we were moving. I thought we were going on vacation, like we had in the past. Nobody consults the baby or tells them the decisions, I guess. SMDH. What tipped me off that we had moved? When my mom enrolled me in school. I was like, "Wait. We're staying here? But it's cold." We had the nerve to move from balmy-all-year-round Ìbàdàn, Nigeria, to Chicago, USA, where the air makes tears run down your face for eight months out of the year.)

Anywho, the first day of school when I walked into my classroom, the teacher asked me to stand in front of all these strange faces and introduce myself. I immediately knew I was too different, and I felt self-conscious in a way I never had before. Who I was and where I was from were too offbeat from what the kids (and even the teacher) in that room were used to. It was my first time walking into a room where not everyone looked like me.

I was sure of nothing. Even the question "What's your name?"

felt like a trap. The answer was Ifeoluwa Ajayi,* but right then and there, nine-year-old me knew that the kids (and the teacher herself) wouldn't pronounce it properly, and they'd make it heavy on their tongues, like it was a burden. My name felt like it was too much. It was too foreign. It was too Nigerian. It was too strange. And it wouldn't do.

I wasn't ashamed, because I am truly proud of my name and love it. But I felt like I needed to protect what is a sacred part of me. So in the three seconds after I was asked, I decided to introduce myself as Lovette instead. It was a nickname that one of my aunts would call me from time to time, because Ifeoluwa means "God's love." (Lovette became Luvvie in college.) Every time afterward, when teachers looked at my original first name on their roll call list and frowned or said "Whew, okay, this one is hard," my decision was affirmed. (They also butchered AJAYI, which is not even a tongue twister but is often turned into one.) The message I kept getting was "This thing about you makes us uncomfortable."

As a Naija girl, I knew the way I spoke was also too strange. The fact that I called a pen a "biro" and cookies "biscuits" weren't my only clues; the first time someone called me an "African booty scratcher" because of how I spoke, I said to myself, "Oh, chick. We

---

*Ifeoluwa Ajayi is pronounced as ee-FEH-oh-LOO-wah ah-jah-YEE, but please don't call me by my first name. It's reserved for the people closest to me. Luvvie will do. (Gotta draw that line. We'll talk more about boundaries in chapter 9.)

gotta lose this accent quick, fast, and in a hurry." So I talked less and listened more to how my classmates spoke. By the time I started high school, I had lost most of the telltale sign that I was new: my Nigerian accent.

The one thing I didn't let go of was my food. I still brought jollof rice for lunch. I briefly tried sandwiches, but I'd be craving spices by the end of lunchtime. So there were times I'd sit in the corner as far from my classmates as possible, to avoid the questions of "What is that smell?" and "What are you eating?" Abeg, face your front and let me enjoy my food in peace.

My heritage, my name, and my mother tongue made me feel too different. And as a teenager in the 1990s, being too distinct from your peers was not cool, so I did my best to not be TOO Nigerian. (I don't know what it's like to be a teenager now, but I will say y'all are WAYYY more accepting of differences than we were. So you're already winning at not being as terrible as we were. CONGRATS!)

Then I got to college, where the best learnings are outside the classroom. It was at the University of Illinois where I reclaimed my Nigerianness. It was there that I met others with stories like mine, who also went by new names to keep theirs from being butchered. It was there that I realized that my perspective, which is very much informed by my culture, was one of my superpowers. It was there that I started the blog that led to the life I live now. It is where I stopped hiding the fact that I love switching back and forth between my mother tongue and English, even in a room full of non-Yorùbás.

Who I am in the world today is an unapologetically Nigerian American, Chicagoan, Black woman. As I inhabit all these identities and seamlessly move through them, that thing that was TOO MUCH about me is a major factor in my success. My humor and writing style are tied to all these parts of me.

If you're reading this, and you are a young Black girl, or an immigrant, or just someone who feels too different, know that I know how you feel. I hope you see me and know that you are not TOO much of who you are. I hope you know that you too can let your tongue take you back to your roots without shame. I hope you know your name is not too distinct. I hope you know you can exist beyond binaries. I hope you know you can thrive and build a life that you want, being exactly who you are at your core. I hope you double down on what makes you different and use it to stand out in the best ways.

Do not allow people to stifle your TOO MUCHness.

Beyoncé is someone who people frequently say is too much. Her audacity. Her love of glittery onesies. Her out-of-this-world performances. Sometimes people get offended at how she dares to be so BIG, but it's clear she knows that ain't her business. Her job is to take up ALL the space she wants when she wants, and it has made her a living icon. It pays off because that is what has allowed her to be the greatest entertainer alive. After her historic Coachella performance, she cemented that title. She then STAMPED it after her incredible visual album *Black Is King*. LIVING ICON.

I think about how Oprah Winfrey is constantly accused of being TOO MUCH for appearing on the cover of *O, The Oprah Magazine* every single month for twenty years (until she decided to stop the print issues). To run a successful magazine is no small feat, but to do it for two decades is the stuff of legends. Thank God she hasn't let people talk her out of what she's known to work.

Michelle Obama's book tour for *Becoming* was in arenas. People thought that was TOO MUCH too. Meanwhile, our Forever FLOTUS was making a whole documentary in those sold-out appearances. The book became a worldwide bestseller. The vision. The boldness. The guts. I'm so here for all of it.

Imagine if any of these women allowed people to convince them that what they wanted or who they were was TOO MUCH. The brilliance we would all be cheated out of would create a vacuum. Imagine if they tried to follow someone else's blueprint to success. We would be missing out on so much magic!

Similarly, you have your own distinct perspective, personality, and purpose. If you let people talk you out of them, everyone misses out on your magic. I get FOMO (fear of missing out), and I really don't wanna think about how much goodness that would keep out of rooms. Fitting in is overrated.

Shout-out to those of us who've been told we are TOO TALK-ATIVE. Or TOO MOUTHY. Some of us are now able to get paid good money for that as professional speakers. Some of us put the words we have in our heads on paper and write books that impact millions around the globe. Our TOO MUCHness can really be beneficial. All it takes is time, opportunity, and consistency.

Whatever it is that people think we are TOO much of comes in handy when it benefits others. However, when it stops being of service to folks' lives and starts making them uncomfortable, that is when it becomes something we should stop. This reaction tells me our TOO MUCHness is clearly useful. That thing that we are too much of is our superpower, and we should wield it with pride.

The person who is considered TOO sensitive is probably someone with a high emotional IQ. They're in tune with how people are feeling, allowing them to detect when a situation will have emotional consequences. They're often really thoughtful about how they speak to other people, and they are the calm in storms. At school, they're the friend who helps mediate fights when everyone gets on each other's nerves.

The person who is TOO uptight is probably the one who is great at being class president. They'll make sure they've noted everyone's concerns and come up with plans to address them. You want them in charge. That type A–ness is extra useful cuz they get things done.

The person who is TOO turnt is the one you will have a great time with at prom. They will help create memories that your future self will smile at.

You might be wondering, "What if people are right if they say

I am TOO something? How do I know I'm not ignoring valid feedback?" Good questions.

I ask myself a few questions when it comes to figuring out what we should consider true and what we should consider trash.

Is this thing getting in the way of my personal growth?

Is this thing hurting someone else?

Is this feedback coming from someone who loves and respects me?

If the answer to all three is no, then wipe your shoulders off, pick your head up, and keep it moving. Otherwise, let's dig deeper on those questions.

IS THIS THING GETTING IN THE WAY OF MY PERSONAL GROWTH?

The thing that people are saying you are TOO much of—does it get in the way of you becoming a better version of yourself? When the thing makes us behave in ways that are not aligned with our core values and are the opposite of the person we wrote about in our mission statements, it is worth taking seriously. I can't say I hold generosity in high regard and then be stingy with my money and time on a regular basis. If I have $100 in my pocket, I see someone who is experiencing homelessness and asking for money, and all I reach for are three pennies I find at the bottom of my purse, then I am not honoring who I said I was. THEN I am probably being TOO stingy.

Am I being TOO hasty and reckless and rigid? Well, do I refuse to change my thoughts and ideas because I think that my way is the only right way? That can interfere with becoming a better person. This probably also means people think of me as an immovable person, which means I'm likely to end up with fewer people who will tell me the truth. That is how people become bullies and tyrants.

Maybe I'm TOO loud, so I'm not encouraging others to be heard in a room I'm in. Maybe I'm always making sure my voice is the only one that is being boosted and not allowing a diversity of ideas to be represented. In those moments, we don't need to stop ourselves or think our ideas aren't necessary. But we can remind ourselves to step back. We can be intentional in knowing when to give space to the collective voice instead of our individual one.

IS THIS THING HURTING SOMEONE ELSE?

Is the thing that I am being scolded about emotionally, mentally, or physically hurtful to someone else? If so, then yes, I should chill and go work on myself. The person who is called too aggressive might need to get their life right if it comes with them being abusive to those around them. There are people who will put hands on other people, even those they say they love. Being physically aggressive mostly comes in handy if you're a professional boxer or an MMA fighter. But a regular human being who is known for constantly fighting other people? That is certainly not who I want to be, and that is not someone I want to be close with. Am I enabling their misbehavior? Will I feel safe around them? Will I be the object of their physical aggression?

Are you being too loud? Yes, you can also definitely be too loud if you're in class, a movie theater, or a library, so please use your inside voice. (Lord knows I don't have any inside voice. I whisper at 90 decibels, but God ain't done working on me yet.)

Does your sensitivity mean you cry anytime you are challenged, therefore using your tears to manipulate others into always giving you your way? There are people who weaponize their tears to avoid accountability. That's not sensitivity but manipulation, which can cause people to resent you because they'll feel like you don't care about their feelings. That's harmful because it says that they do not matter.

Sometimes when white women and girls cry, it can literally put Black people in jeopardy. Picture it: A white girl feels challenged or uncomfortable about something a Black person said or did. Instead of using her words, she cries. Instantly, no matter what caused the situation, she ends up being pampered. We've seen white girl tears shut down conversations, even if she started the drama. The other person? Ends up being scolded. Or fired. Or arrested. Or killed. That's what happened to Emmett Till. A white woman's tears got him killed.

So, yes, times like those can lead to someone else's harm. That is when you check yourself and do better.

We need to be clear about when we are being TOO to a fault.

If whatever you are being accused of is not silencing somebody who has less social access than you, then what is the real accusation? We've all been in rooms with really loud dudes who won't use the shutthehellup coupon code, and what they do is create chaos with no purpose. But when people accuse you of being loud, is it in the times when you are speaking for somebody who doesn't have a voice? Is it when people would prefer that you let something that isn't fair thrive? In those times, you aren't being too loud. What you are being is too inconvenient for that room. You've made that room uncomfortable by doing the right thing. Keep doing the right thing.

IS THIS FEEDBACK COMING FROM SOMEONE WHO LOVES AND RESPECTS ME?

If the "too much" is coming from someone you aren't sure has your best interests at heart or who has been hypercritical of you in the past, then it might not be something you should internalize. I surround myself with people I trust and love and who aren't afraid to pull my card. When THEY tell me I am being TOO something (like stubborn, stern, thoughtless), I reflect, process what they've said, and then figure out how I can do better and show up better next time.

If it's coming from someone who is a troll or a known hater or even someone who might be going through their own drama, I have to side-eye it. This is especially useful in the age of social media, where thousands of people can make judgments on who we are at any given point. Imagine a tweet that goes viral, that has people you will never know and who don't care about you coming at you recklessly. As they are telling you you're TOO something, you will need someone close to you to vouch for that thing for it to really matter.

But here's the thing. Sometimes the people who tell us we are TOO something are those who love us dearly and want the best for us. They can be people who are closest to us (parents, friends, teachers) who really do adore the ground we walk on. They mean us well, but sometimes we hear "You are TOO _____" from them. It is possible that they are trying to protect us by making that judgment, but they can be projecting their own insecurities onto us in the process.

You have a mother who is more of a quiet type? She might have told you she thinks you need to be more calm or to stop being so loud all the time. We've had family members tell us we're too skinny in an attempt to make sure we are eating as we should be, but it comes across as shaming of our bodies. And shout-out to all the aunties who have greeted someone with "You're putting on too much weight" or "You're getting too fat." They mean well, but the road to hell is paved with good intentions.

Many a kinfolk or friend has created inferiority complexes in people they love with their words that we're TOO something. And instead of letting their lack of chill slide off our backs, we take it to heart. It's not our fault, because the people who can hurt us the most are those we love the most.

This third question should not be considered without the first two, because if we ALWAYS take on what our family and friends say about us, even though the thing they said does not hinder our personal growth or hurt anyone, we'll be walking replicas of them. Or we'll spend our lives trying to measure up to the person they THINK we should be. We'll be constantly trying to win their validation, instead of constantly trying to make sure we're growing. And lemme tell you, that is exhausting.

Someone called you too tall? Do they not understand that it means they are less likely to need a step stool when you're around? Don't they realize that you can always see above folks at the concert so you can help narrate what's happening onstage? Plus, you probably take amazing group selfies because your arm has reach. Who needs a selfie stick? Not you!

Someone thinks you're too bold? It means you get anyone's attention, and that comes in handy in a crowded room. It means you aren't easy to forget, and that is charisma.

Someone thinks you're too emotional? It means when you're about to get written up for detention, you can probably cry on cue and make the teacher feel guilty enough to give you a warning.

I'm kidding. Don't do it. I won't help get you out of trouble. HA!

So what should you do? BE TOO MUCH. And do not apologize for it. If your TOO MUCHness is not obstructing your personal evolution or actually hurting someone else, stand in it.

Notice I said PERSONAL evolution. Out in the world, there is A LOT hanging on us being as un-different from what is expected as possible. School teaches us how to think alike, dress alike, talk alike. Social media tells us what's trendy so we can do it just like everyone else. We are taught that being TOO different is not welcome, so basing ourselves and our worthiness on everyone else's fickle thoughts will lead us astray time and time again. Trying to fit in will frustrate us because things change constantly. What's considered popular today is passé tomorrow. Ain't it exhausting???

At school, we come across a lot of people with a lot of feelings. Oftentimes, you are doing your homework AND the work of babysitting other people's feelings. That in itself is how a great deal of people get convinced that they are TOO MUCH. If we base whether we are TOO MUCH on our friends or on social media, we will forever be too much. I think about the Black girls who have to show up to school after doing amazing work, in spite of teachers and classmates who label them as TOO smart or TOO intimidating. I see you, young sis who knows she's smarter than everyone in that class but has to nod and smile so she isn't considered aggressive. I see you, person who shows up with straightened hair so she won't be considered too Black for that school where she's the ONLY one who looks like her in those hallways. You are doing your best, and I hope one day you find yourself in a place where you don't feel like you have to wear these types of masks to get through the day. I'm proud of you.

Oh, and I hope you know that popularity in high school has zero effect on how happy your life ends up being as a grown-up. In fact, a lot of us see the people we knew to be popular in high school and notice they are super tired and washed out now. Being uncool right now comes in handy because the only way you go from here is UP. Also, you'll be part of an elite club of "people who were really uncool when they were younger and grew up to be dope-ass people who run shit." Hold on to that for the days when you're feeling especially down.

So to everyone who has been told they are too much, that they are excessive in some way, and been made to feel like their extra-ness or weirdness means they aren't enough, I see you. I feel you. I am you. So what do I do? I insist on being me. The totality of me. And then I add some extra me-ness.

Sometimes I add some extra ME seasoning on myself when I step into a room, because I want people to get used to looking at someone walking in, maybe not in a package they expect, doing good work, and being excellent. And LOVING herself as she does it.

I am often invited to speak at conferences or at major companies, and when I ask what the dress code is, I'm usually told business casual. Look, I LOVE blazers and oxfords and wing tips. Forty percent of the time, I dress like an old white man from Maine who owns a yacht. My closet is full of the finest in preppy clothes. However, there are times when I will ignore the dress code on purpose for the sake of being too different. Why? So people know that we belong, in all our forms, in whatever uniform we show up in.

Once, when I arrived at a tech conference I was hosting, the room was full of Chads and Everetts (white nerdy dudes). I was one of two Black people in the room. I showed up the next day wearing a shirt that had Lionel Richie on it, with the words HELLO, IS IT ME YOU'RE LOOKING FOR? Because the host they expected probably wasn't me, but there I was anyway. Bloop!

I know that not everyone has the social freedom to always be a rebel with a cause. And I'm not here to make you feel some type of way about doing your best. Instead, I want you to keep your head above water in a world that might feel like it is trying to drown you. Do what you can when and where you can. Don't beat yourself up. You deserve grace.

I am, however, here to let you know that you aren't alone in being told you are TOO MUCH. And there isn't anything wrong with you. I'm encouraging you to think about the times you have downplayed yourself to try to make other people comfortable. I want you to reflect on the times you have been made to feel like you do not belong or you do not measure up or your presence is somehow a nuisance because you are a highlighter in a sea of pencils.

You will always be too much for somebody. You wanna be smaller? Sure, you can try. Some people will still consider your attempt not good enough. You turned your ten down to an eight when they were looking for a four. Why even try? Just give them the full ten. We can bend ourselves till we break trying to conform. And I promise you there will still be someone who is not satisfied. Fitting in is overrated.

Your TOO MUCHness is a superpower, and haters don't wanna see you don your cape. So what do you do? Be so much. Be the full totality of you. Add some extra to the you-ness. Be TOO MUCH, because no matter what you do and how hard you try, someone somewhere will still think you are TOO something. You #MinusWell (might as well) give them real reason to think so.

Be the Youest You That Ever Youed.

3

DREAM AUDACIOUSLY

We fear having too much hope.

 The world can sometimes feel like the headquarters of Mayhem Enterprises, breaking our hearts into pieces every day with chaos and madness. We get disappointed often with tragedies and horrific news, living in constant suspense, not knowing when these things will happen to us. Pandora's box is forever opening.

So I get why we are afraid of dreaming of what we want. It's hard for us to get our hopes up that things will go the way we want them to. Yet, and still, we need to put this worry as far away from our minds as possible. You might call it madness, but I call it necessary.

When we are afraid of having too much hope, we're actually

afraid of being disappointed. We are anxious about expecting the world to be gentle with us, because what if we end up flat on our faces? So we dream small or not at all. Because if we expect nothing or expect something small, we cannot be disappointed when the big things don't happen. We think it's a great way to protect ourselves, but it's really a liability on our lives, because we are constantly bracing for impact. When we are afraid of thinking things can be too good, it can become a self-fulfilling prophecy. We think life, in all its struggle, is waiting to punch us in the neck and go "OH, YOU THOUGHT I WAS GONNA BE GOOD TO YOU?" so we don't dream because we don't even wanna give it the satisfaction. We wanna stay ready so we ain't gotta get ready.

This shows up in real life when we might not apply to the school we wanna go to because we think we have no chance of being admitted. Or we won't try out for that sport because we already expect that we won't make it onto the team. We might not say hey to our crush because we're expecting to be rejected. But what if we would have met a life helper or landed that perfect internship that would have led to the job of our dreams? Basically, we end up living colorless versions of the lives we truly want, which then confirms that life is crappy.

Here's the thing. Life can absolutely be a complicated filth bucket that is unfair even for people who TRY and STRIVE and DREAM. The difference is that those people can go to sleep at night and wake up in the morning knowing that they at least tried. They can have some small relief that they did what they could. Life's shenanigans can be off-the-chart levels for them. But they blame life, not themselves, because they tried. They dreamed anyway.

M any of us don't know how to dream, since we live in a world that makes it really hard if you're not white, male, straight, Christian, able-bodied, and cisgender. We've been bound by oppressive systems that are designed to not give us an inch, even when we earn a mile. We have been shunned and disrespected and erased from the things we are entitled to. We are constantly living in default survival mode, so dreaming is a privilege and an allowance we haven't been able to afford. Imagination is also a benefit that has been yanked from us, because shit ain't fair. Glass ceilings have shown us that all we'll do by wanting more is continue to hit our heads on limits. So we wake up one day having been stripped of the very hope we need if we're gonna have a fighting chance at anything resembling equity in this world.

I want to dream like white men who have never been told there are ceilings for them, let alone skies. I think about the story of Summit and Powder Mountain.*

What's Summit, you ask? It's an invite-only social organization

---

*Alyson Shontell, "It's Official: 4 Young Founders Just Bought a $40 Million Mountain to Party On," *Business Insider*, May 7, 2013, https://www.businessinsider.com /what-summit-series-is-and-why-it-bought-40-million-powder-mountain-for-summit -eden-young to20135.

that has its headquarters on the mountain it owns (Powder Mountain). Let me repeat: an organization has property on a mountain that it has spent money on. DID YOU KNOW MOUNTAINS ARE UP FOR SALE??? Because I surely didn't.

Nah, let's talk about THAT. I'll give you the tl;dr (too long; didn't read), simplified version of the story. Summit started because a group of white guys would invite their friends for weekends in cabins on a mountain they liked in Utah. Then they started going to this mountain more frequently. So they thought, "Wait, since we're here so often, why don't we buy the mountain and invite more of our friends? Let's make this a thing." And they did just that, buying Powder Mountain for $40 million and getting others to invest in their dream.

I have a few questions that I'd love to ask them:

- How did the conversation about buying the mountain even go?

- Did anyone laugh at the first person who brought up the idea?

- Were they all high, and on what?

- When they reached "Okay, let's buy the mountain" consensus, were they afraid of this idea?

- Who do you call when you're looking to buy a mountain? I know there's no yellow pages listing for that. (Meanwhile, I know I just dated myself with that reference. If you don't know what the yellow pages are, that's okay. Google it and laugh at us.)

The point stands: these men thought to buy a mountain and actually did it. If WE were to go on vacation, and had a great time, we might think about buying a mug to commemorate it. If we wanted to really do it big, we might even ask about buying the mattress we slept on because it was so comfortable. These men thought about buying the mountain! We have been oppressed into having mattress dreams, while they have been privileged into mountain dreams. Wow.

The audacity of unshackled white men is massive. The only way I wish to be more like them is by having the lack of oppression that gives me the freedom, gumption, and unmitigated gall to think it's even possible to own a mountain. I want that dauntless- ness. The system that white men created, designed, and profit from—that makes the rest of us afraid of our own shadow while they step on our backs—is well done, ain't it? It works so well.

This must be said: It's not that the men of Summit are smarter or even braver than anyone else for thinking about buying a moun- tain. No. I mean, they are smart, but they (like millions of white men) benefit from being constantly centered, elevated, and catered to, so they have not been programmed to expect less from the world, like the rest of us have. Why would they not think of owning a mountain?

We need the nerve and rashness to dare to think these things are possible for us too, even when we know that we might need to be four times as good, three times as qualified, and twice as professional to get what they will have handed to them when they walk into a room in their cargo shorts, half-asleep. So I say with this caveat and without naïveté: dreaming big is in itself a privilege. However, I'm asking us to trick ourselves into thinking we have the privilege of dreaming big.

Being audacious enough to dream means discovering the courage to think your life can be bigger than you can even imagine. You might not be sure what your dreams really are right now, and that's okay. You're young, and you don't have to have it all figured out yet. In fact, you don't have to have much figured out. As you embark on this life journey, you'll get more and more clarity. You might have a dream now that doesn't end up being your dream in two years. That is perfectly fine, because lemme tell you. The adults around you who look like they got everything together? It took a while. It took a lot of trial and a lot of error. But I wanna start getting you to hear that you GOTTA dream boldly. You have to. Dream the mountain dreams. Often, we don't get there because we are afraid of what will happen if hope doesn't pan out. We fear how disappointed or heartbroken we will be.

That is why we have to take the risk and think that what we want to happen is even possible in the first place. Dreaming is a gesture of courage in itself, because to think of the life we want is to be bold enough to think someway and somehow, it could come to pass.

On my journey as an accidental writer, author, and speaker, there have been a lot of times I was afraid to dream too big, because I didn't wanna be let down. But other times, when something happened, I realized it was because I had actually spoken that hope out loud, even if only to myself. Let me tell you a bit more about how I got here.

Growing up, I knew exactly what I wanted to be: Doctor Luvvie was the dream, because I was nerdish and I wanted to help people—you know, the hope of immigrant and first-gen kids everywhere. A lot of the adults around me said it over and over again, "You're gonna be a doctor one day," and I believed them. So when we moved to the United States from Nigeria, that dream was one of the few things I brought with me.

Throughout my academic career, I didn't have to try hard to get As. I would write all my papers the night before they were due or the morning of and get As. But when I started college at the

University of Illinois as a psychology premed major, Chemistry 101 happened to me. I think a lot of dreams have died in a science class. HA!

I attended that class every day and went to office hours with my professor and teacher's aide, but it was an utter struggle. At the end of the semester, I got my grade: a solid D!!! D for Don't. D for "Doctor Dream is Dead." It was the first D (which I considered a failure) of my academic career, and I definitely sobbed like someone had burned my pot of rice.

After having a come-to-Jesus moment with myself like "Sis, you don't even like hospitals. You'd be the worst doctor ever!" I went to my advisor and dropped premed, deciding I'd probably do better pursuing my psychology degree and getting my master's in industrial/organizational psych. I could still help people that way. YAY, ME!

(Fun fact: I didn't tell my mom that I had dropped the premed part of my major, so three and a half years later when she came to graduation, she was like, "Okay, so where's the premed graduation?" Me: "See, what had happened was . . . I got this D in chemistry. I dropped that dream very quickly. But hey, I finished college in four years! YAY, ME!" Clearly, I was an everlasting vagabond. I think at that point, my mom was basically thinking that since I got out of college and ain't nobody call her about me getting in trouble or acting a complete fool, it was my life. She trusted me with me, which was a gift, because that could have turned out badly. HEY,

YOUNG PEOPLE READING THIS, DON'T TELL THIS LIE OF OMISSION TO YOUR PARENTS. I will not be held liable for it. Cool? Cool.)

As my doctor dream was ending, another was beginning. My friends peer-pressured me into starting a "weblog." And by "peer-pressured" I mean I'm pretty sure I only needed one suggestion and I was into it. I started my first blog in early 2003; it was titled something emo like *Consider This the Letter I Never Wrote*. In it, I documented my whole college career, writing about exams I wasn't studying for, the D I got, roommate problems. The blog used Comic Sans font, so you know it was a mess. But I loved this new hobby, and my psychology classes too. I did a few marketing internships and realized I was good at marketing too (and I liked it).

When I graduated in 2006, I deleted that undergrad blog and started what is now AwesomelyLuvvie.com. New life, new blog! I'd work my nine-to-five job in marketing, but when I came home, I'd blog. As I wrote about the world and how I saw it, word of my blog spread, and in 2009, I won my first award: Best Humor Blog in the now-defunct Black Weblog Awards. I was geeked because here I was getting recognition for my hobby.

Hobby. Yeah, okay.

Get this. I was afraid to call myself a writer. WRITER? WHERE? I was afraid of that title and all the dreams that could come from it that I would be unable to fulfill. Toni Morrison and Maya Angelou and Zora Neale Hurston. Those were writers. I was just a girl who put up blog posts talking about whatever was on my spirit. Writer? "Girl, bye. You can't measure up to that title." That's what I told myself.

I liked my job as a marketing coordinator. I was making enough to pay my bills, which weren't many. I was fine. Except I wasn't. I was bored with the job, and I felt restless. But I wasn't going to quit. Nah, we don't do that. We will just swallow down the discomfort and keep clocking in every day.

What I should have remembered is that whole honesty-as-my-core-value thing. When I refuse to be honest with myself, the lies I try to tell, even to myself, don't go well. My work ethic is one of my strongest traits, but I started being a terrible employee. I would show up to work and give my some, not my all. I'd update my blog at my desk. And one day, I even fell asleep at a staff meeting. Like full-on, eyes closed, head dropped. In a meeting of nine people. BRUHHH. As an employee, I was being increasingly trash.

In April 2010, I was suddenly laid off. They said it was due to budget cuts. I had the nerve to be surprised, y'all. The gall to feel like I'd been blindsided. Sis, you've been a rubbish employee for months! In fact, they did me a favor by laying me off when they would have been justified in firing me.

That layoff/firing was God and the universe pushing me to take a leap of faith to stand in this writer dream I was too scared to have. But I'm a stubborn goat, so I didn't see it as that. Instead, I was sending out my résumés left and right because I needed my biweekly paychecks and insurance! This shoe habit was not going to keep itself up, after all.

During that time, I'd wonder if I needed to stop putting so much time into my blog, but I couldn't quit. Something wouldn't let me. I still didn't consider it anything but my part-time hobby, when all signs were pointing to the fact that my purpose was to use my written words to make people laugh and think critically, and to make the world better.

I was a writer. But I was afraid, because there was no real blueprint for me to follow, and I didn't feel like it was a tangible-enough profession. To make money as I job-hunted, I designed websites and consulted with small businesses and other bloggers to teach them how to tell their stories using social media (my specialty).

After over a year of looking for a traditional job (and still blogging), I finally got hired for a full-time position as the social media manager for a global food brand. I went into the office on that first day, decked out in my "I'm serious" business-casual slacks and a button-down. My first task was to create a PowerPoint presentation for a campaign, and I was in there knocking it out! Then came 1:00 p.m. and the walls of that building started closing in on me. Isweartogawd I wanted to slide off my nice ergonomic chair onto the floor and lie there. My spirit was not gelling with this new job. That night, I wrote an email to my new boss. I thanked them for the job and notified them that it was my first day AND my last. Bless it, but I couldn't do it.

In the meantime, other opportunities continued to pour in, all related to my writing. I finally started wondering why I was so afraid of calling myself a writer.

A few months later, I was credentialed to do press coverage on the red carpet and backstage at the Academy Awards (February 2012). I was chosen because a producer who loved my blog thought I should be there. There I was, in my role as Awesomely Luvvie, backstage at the Oscars, eating Wolfgang Puck's shrimp and chocolates, next to journalists from the BBC, CNN, *Entertainment Tonight*! Me. A whole me! WOW.

That experience shifted my world: I was in that room and breathing that air because of my gift, because of my words. How was I NOT a writer? I might not be Toni or Maya, but I was Luvvie, and the fear of the writer title had kept me from truly honoring my purpose. Fear can very concretely keep us from doing and saying the things that are our purpose. But when I made the decision that I was not going to let fear rule my life or dictate what I do, my wildest dreams started coming true.

After college, I had two big dreams that I put down on paper numerous times, through vision statements I wrote and random "life bucket lists" I made over the years. One was to write a *New York Times* bestselling book. The other was to help my mom retire one day. As a single mother, Yemi Ajayi has always been one of my prime motivations to soar in this world. The sacrifices she made—moving us to the United States and leaving everything behind, somehow managing to make a dollar out of ten cents—allowed me to dream. And she did it with such grace that I didn't even know that we were usually one paycheck away from being out on the streets. We did not have money and were barely making it. I just didn't know it.

I've wanted to make my mother proud with my life, and I've wanted her last decades on this earth to be as worry free as possible.

When I turned thirty in 2015, I decided it was going to be my year of "Afraid? Do it anyway." I was going to pursue anything that scared me or that I wouldn't typically do. That was the year I went skydiving, when I traveled solo to five countries, and when I wrote my first book. I climbed that personal mountain and poured out seventy-five thousand words that became *I'm Judging You: The Do-Better Manual*. I finally could write that book because I overcame my fear of calling myself a writer. The courage I needed didn't come from a special class I took or some diploma I got. It was literally a shift in how I was thinking. The monster didn't stop being so big. I just decided to fight it. The dragon didn't go away on its own; I had to slay it.

I'm Judging You was published on September 13, 2016, and on September 21, I got the phone call that it had hit the *New York Times* bestseller list at number five. I was officially in a club that came with special privileges, and my life instantly changed. The fees I charged for work I did doubled, and doors opened for me that I hadn't even known existed, which led to my other major dream being realized.

A month later, I called my mother and told her she could stop working because I could now handle the bills for BOTH of us. It was the biggest pleasure of my life to be able to show her that all her work and sacrifices were not in vain. My book hitting the *New York Times* bestseller list allowed me to tell my mom to retire. And that dream led me to the opportunity to write my second book, dedicated to Yemi's mother, my grandmother Fúnmiláyọ̀.

It all began with a blog from a girl who thought she wanted to be a doctor but was really a writer. But she was afraid of that title, and what failing at it could look like. Then God was like, "My hardheaded child, I got plans for you. Trust me. Rest in it." And after my stubborn ass ran out of excuses and dared to use the title that scared me, things began to fall into place in a way that felt divine.

I was afraid because I couldn't find an example of a writer like me, but I became that example for myself. And because of that, I am now that example for other people. We are prone to thinking that if we haven't seen what we want, in the exact form we imagine it in, then it isn't possible. To those of you who wanna become writers one day, I hope you can tell your parents that. "I want to be a writer, and I can do it because look at Luvvie. She's done it and so can I."

Oftentimes, when we want something we don't see the path to, we are afraid of it, because we could lose our way since there's no map. Well, maybe WE are supposed to draw the map so someone who comes behind us won't get lost. Create the map you didn't have. That's what I did. We must give ourselves permission to be who we want to be, even if we don't have the blueprint yet, and that starts with dreaming.

It is truly a blessing to be able to speak my dreams, even if only to myself, and see how they have been realized. I know there's no magical dream fairy that grants wishes. And I don't necessarily claim luck in this either. I think I've seen some of my wildest dreams come true because I've put in a lot of hard work. I also give credit to God's grace, because I know there are people more talented than me or people who work harder than me whose names we will never know.

But I am always hopeful. While we may voice our wants, we may not always get what we dreamed of, in the exact form we dreamed of it. However, it is important to continue to dream, even in the midst of disappointment, because it opens up our minds and lets us see things bigger.

And above all, your dreams deserve to be yours. When I grew up thinking I wanted to be a doctor, I didn't realize that it was because I had been TOLD that I would become a doctor by the grown-ups in my life. I had spent eighteen years hearing that I would make a great doctor, so I took that on.

The people who love us want the best for us, but sometimes they want THEIR best for us, imposing their hopes and dreams on us in the process. They might not even be doing it purposefully.

There are countless people walking around right now who are living the lives their parents dictated instead of what they wanted. How many people have lost the loves of their lives because their parents didn't approve? How many people are in careers they absolutely hate because that is what they were told to do? How many people are miserable today cuz of choices their parents made on their behalf that they never said no to?

Your dreams deserve to be yours, because your purpose is not a group activity. You were not put on this earth to fulfill your parents' or anyone else's dreams for you, or to relive their lives to redo the things they failed at.

I'm here to tell you that you can say NO to everyone else's expectations if and when they don't match yours. DISAPPOINT YOUR PARENTS if it means you are choosing YOURSELF. Let them be upset at you. Because at the end of your life, you will be the one contending with a lifetime of self-betrayal and misery for their validation (which may still never come).

We were born to pursue purpose, not people-please. That means we deserve to live the life we want to live, charting our own path, no matter what our parents want for us.

DISAPPOINT YOUR PARENTS.

DISAPPOINT THEIR EXPECTATIONS (if they aren't aligned with your own).

DISAPPOINT THEIR DREAMS FOR YOU (if they don't match yours).

HONOR YOURSELF. Disappoint whoever you have to. Betray yourself less.

The lives we live are full of people's dreams realized. The things we use every day are born from the audacity of someone who thought it was possible. There are many times when I'm traveling and I'm in awe of the fact that I'm in a tin can in the sky. When I'm eye level with clouds and think, "Bruhhh, whose great-great-great-great-grandparent would have thought this was possible?" That feels magical. Science is made up of imaginations that ran wild and dreamed magical things that actually became achievable.

So why don't we operate our lives in this way?

I often think about all that my grandmother overcame to

become the fierce woman I ended up knowing, like being orphaned at seventeen and having to start life over. That woman, born in 1931, ended up doing things and creating beings that led to me. Through her dreaming that her life could be what she wanted, I am here today, standing on her shoulders. Her existence convinces me to let my imagination run wild. So I owe it to Fúnmiláyọ̀ Fáloyin to think of pies in the sky with my name on them.

When we dream, we're giving others permission to do the same.

When our dreams are big, we're telling the folks who know us that they don't have to be small either.

When our dreams come true, we're expanding the worlds of others because now they know theirs can too.

We must dream and dream boldly and unapologetically.

If we do not give ourselves permission to dream, how do we give ourselves permission to thrive? So give yourself the allowance to think about that thing that feels too big and too far to touch. Dream of the mountain, not just of the mattress.

Life's adventures never promise a straight path, and that's often what stops us. But we must dream. All we have, even in the worst moments, are the dreams of better things to come.

4

OWN YOUR DOPENESS

We fear being perceived as arrogant.

 We spend time trying to be humble and modest because we've been told that to do otherwise is to think we're superior to others. We dedicate a lot of time to trying to make sure that nobody can accuse us of being too proud. A part of me is all, "Yes, let's keep perspective and stay grounded." Another part of me is like, "HUMILITY CAN GO TO HELL. LET THESE FOLKS HAVE IT."

Sometimes you gotta show up, show out, and let people know that you have arrived, so they gotta make room.

There is an oft-posted quote that says, "Carry yourself with the confidence of a mediocre white man." In the previous chapter, I talked about having some of their gumption, but I don't wanna carry myself in the way they do it cuz that confidence is bland AF. It might be ballsy, but it doesn't come with much swag. Instead, I want us to carry ourselves with the confidence of an older West African woman who has been through some things, come through on the other side, and doesn't look like what she's been through. A thousand useless goats can't tell them nothing.

M y grandma was the queen of Smell the Roses while Here. What does that mean? It means that woman was not shy about accepting any and all love sent her way. Growing up with her, I saw what it was like to be unapologetic about how awesome you are. It wasn't that she was arrogant or went around to people declaring how amazing she was. Nah. She didn't have to. But others made sure they told her how incredible she was. And not only did she say thank you, she also sat in the compliment and let it fill her heart up. She didn't run from it, make excuses for it, or diminish herself in an attempt to seem as humble as she was supposed to be.

Mama Fáloyin loved the Lord with all her heart. And like many Black grandmas around the diaspora, she had a main line directly to Jesus and His Holy Posse. So, on Sundays, where would you find her? In church, of course. She was a staunch Christian, and specifically a member of a denomination called Cherubim and Seraphim (C&S). Actually, correction: she was a prophetess at the church. Okay, no. I'm not giving her all the glory yet. Her official title was the Most Senior Mother-in-Israel Prophetess Fáloyin. I want you to read that again. My grandma had a certificate from the church crowning her as THE MOST Senior Mother-in-Israel Prophetess Fáloyin. I laugh about how things and people do the most, but she literally WAS the most. I don't even know what that whole title actually means, but if there's one thing Nigerians love, it is grand titles. The longer, the better. The more grandiose, the better.

Members of the C&S church wore white gowns (sultanas), prioritized praise and worship, and therefore spent five hours at each church service. My grandma herself contributed to making each service at least thirty minutes longer. Lemme tell you why.

Service started at 10:00 a.m. Praise and worship went on for about thirty minutes. Then Grandma would show up at around 10:30 a.m. (Because why should she be on time? A WHOLE her.) When the pastor and choir learned that she was outside and ready to come in, EVERYTHING stopped. I'm talking record scratch. Stop the presses, and stop the singing. Her presence was then announced to the church as the doors opened, and a welcome committee met her to usher her in.

Then music started playing, and my grandma, like the perpetual holy bride of Christ that she was, made her way down the aisle dancing. As if that wasn't extra enough, Grandma would dance five steps forward but stop to take two steps back, for true peppering and scattering! She took her sweet time, and the mini carnival lasted all the way down the massive church till she took her place at the pew in the first row, at the seat only she could occupy. If doing the most was a sport, that lady was a Hall of Famer. Entrance theme music? Welcome committee? Interruption of services? Dancing for your life? CHECK CHECK CHECK CHECK.

The church insisted on doing this regularly, and Granny, not being shy, protested minimally. She reveled in it. And that in itself is revolutionary behavior in a world where you are not encouraged to celebrate yourself.

We do not all get a weekly celebration of our very presence via song and dance, but there is something to be said for how we would handle it if it ever came. Many of us don't even know how to accept compliments. Someone tells us our shoes are cute and we're quick to go, "These? Please. I just pulled them out the back of the closet," when a simple "Thank you" could go a long way. People might tell us, "You look amazing," and we go, "Nah, you." There is, of course, nothing wrong with exchanging compliments, but how often do we do it just because we are uncomfortable with being praised? How often do WE praise ourselves after doing something great? How often do we sit in the good vibes of someone SEEING us, acknowledging it, and sending some words to prove it? We don't get a gift for being the most self-deprecating in a room. Or being the one who can make fun of ourselves best. We have mastered that. Now I want us to master the art of owning our dopeness.

What I learned from my grandmother is how to allow myself to be truly celebrated. Girls, especially, have been told that humility is a required character trait. And somehow, that humility has been turned into perpetual self-deprecation. We've been convinced that the more we downplay our awesomeness, the better the world is. As if knowing we're majestic is somehow a threat to the climate. As if accepting celebration of our wondrous ways makes gas prices go up. As if knowing we wake up and piss excellence is a cause of world hunger.

This permeates everything we do and how we move through the world. When you are not used to owning your dopeness, odds are you're actually covering up how amazing you are. We're not hyping ourselves up like we should, and how does that show up? It means we end up selling ourselves short.

Some of us struggle with telling our friends and family our accomplishments and good news because it seems like we're bragging. But your achievements are factual things. Not speaking about them doesn't mean they didn't happen. And you know what? If speaking about them makes someone feel like you're bragging, so what? AND SO? Then consider me a Bragger Extraordinaire!

You post or send a text about something you've done well. And the person who sees it on social or receives it rolls their eyes at you because you did well. Or they unfollow you. Or they delete your number. Is that someone you actually want in your life? Is that the person you want to sit next to you every day? Is that the person you want to invite to your home? No? Okay then, why do they matter? Why do their thoughts about you actually make a difference? And then, what if this is someone you actually do not know at all and have never met, and they are mad and call you arrogant because you keep winning? What does this person have to do with you? Should this stranger be the reason you now keep your leveling up to yourself? Is this person the one who will stop you from celebrating yourself?

NO.

Do not let people make you feel bad for doing well, and for being you, and for being amazing, and for being accomplished. If someone gets upset at you for announcing something you did, that person is not your people. Those people do not deserve your dopeness. And those people should serve no important role in your life. You don't need enemies of progress around you.

Let's be real. Standing unapologetically in how good you are and how worthy you are will have some people not liking you. Because sometimes we reflect other people's shortcomings. We are a mirror of their failures. If they're not doing well, but we are, it might rub them the wrong way. And because of that, we will be the target of disdain because people want that confidence and resent it in us. It's not about you walking around and bragging that you got an A while everyone else got an F. But it's that you are not supposed to hide your good work simply to make others feel better about their failure. If you're good at science, telling someone "I guess I'm just okay" doesn't honor you. Tell them, "Yeah, I've figured out biology. Lemme know if I can be of help to you."

Owning your dopeness is not about being liked (or disliked) by others. It's really about being liked by yourself first and foremost. One of my favorite proverbs is "When there is no enemy within, the enemy outside can do you no harm." If you are strong in yourself, the actions of everyone else are less likely to move you. Remember we talked about that in chapter 1.

I want you to think YOU are great, cuz there are really terrible people who think they're amazing. And people believe them strictly because they've convinced others of it. Knowing that there are subpar and mediocre-ass people out there who think they deserve all the good in the world and want heaps of praise, when your EXCEPTIONAL ass is questioning yourself at every corner, makes me wanna fight the air. Trust and believe that there are people with far fewer skills than you who cannot be swayed from thinking that a party should be thrown in their honor every day. People who cannot hold a torch to you are out here crowning themselves.

Never underestimate the effect of confidence. If you believe you're the dopest thing walking, you might convince people of the same, just because you're so headstrong about it as a fact.

It's time to accept we're incredible specimens. You do not have to wear a T-shirt saying I'M THE GREATEST OF ALL TIME. I'm not saying be a doûche about it, but I am saying we err on the side of humility to our detriment. I want you to take up space, without apology. DO. NOT. SHRINK. We've had so much practice shrinking ourselves and trying to make ourselves smaller that when it's time for us to take up space, we don't even know how. Even when we are called, we run. Even when we are celebrated, we tell people it's too much. Even when we're told to speak, we use a whisper. Why? Who are we helping by being muted versions of ourselves?

Some of us not only make ourselves smaller but apologize for our very being. We actually say sorry for our presence, as if we exist as some sort of transgression to others. We say sorry when someone passes us on a sidewalk, as if both of us don't have a right to be there at once. We even say sorry for our FACES. I've seen people write on social media about a picture they posted, "Sorry that my face looks like it does." Wait. You are asking people for forgiveness for your visage? HOW? WHY? What did your face do to them?

But I get it. A lot of it is tied to how we might have been treated in the past. Maybe we were bullied at school. Maybe we've gotten trolls running to our social media posts to say horrific things. The world has thrown enough daggers at us that holes might remain. This isn't the book that will help you break through that (because that is a book in and of itself). I simply ask that you stop apologizing for your existence and for the things attached to your body. Even if you feel like you should, I am here to tell you that you should not.

You do not have to apologize for your vitality. You should not apologize for who you are. Your existence does not warrant apology but warrants celebration. The world is better off because you are here.

It makes me so sad that we do this, especially girls and women.

Somewhere along the way, they told us our glitter was ashes. They told us that what we touched turned to dust, not gold. They convinced us that we bled as punishment, not purpose fulfillment. Somewhere along the way, our magic was minimized. They said we were ordinary, not walking proof of miracles. And we started believing them. We did. We let the world tell us we had to apologize for ourselves. We had to be polite but not stern, sexy but not too sexual, bosses but not bossy, confident but not cocky, motherly but not matronly. We had to hide the rough edges they created in us and be soft but not fluffy.

And Black girls and women? Well, we've been told we're the mule when we are the mother of all of this. We are jewels. We are the reason for poems to be written, sappy love notes with metaphors that seem hyperbolic but are more grounded in truth than you know.

Somewhere along the way, we were told we weren't enough

when we are truly EVERYTHING. We are literally LIFE ever-lasting. We are God's vessel. Science can't explain us. We are magic. Don't let nobody tell you a damb thing. You're made of pixie dust. They just don't know what to do with it.

N ot owning my dopeness almost had me missing out on a major blessing and honor. Lemme tell you that story.

In the beginning of 2016, I was getting ready for the year of *I'm Judging You*. My first book was going to be released in September, so at the top of the year I was focused on that.

In March, I got an email from the Oprah Winfrey Network (OWN) team, congratulating me for being chosen as part of Oprah's inaugural SuperSoul100 list. It was a list of one hundred people who Oprah thought were "elevating humanity." I read the email and basically laughed because I just knew it had to be spam. This must be from the same Nigerian prince who said he had a $342 million inheritance for me. LMAO. Good one.

Then I got a text from someone who works at an agency that works with the OWN team to tell me to check my email for something important. I was like, "Wait. Was that email real??" I had to go into my spam folder to retrieve it. Sure enough, it was legit. I had been chosen as one of a hundred people who Oprah thought were doing some dope things in this world. BRUHHHHH, lemme just lie here in disbelief.

After I managed to close my mouth and call a few people I love while squealing, I finally read the email in detail and saw I was invited to a SuperSoul100 brunch, just for those who Lady O had chosen.

When I showed up, I was sitting at a table with Sophia Bush. I looked over at the next table and saw Ava DuVernay and Arianna Huffington. Then I looked across the room, which was on the OWN lot, and saw Janet Mock and Zendaya. I was truly floored. In my head, I kept yelling, "How did I get here amongst these giants? HOOWWWW? Was a mistake made?"

No mistake was made. You're dope. You're in the room. Own it. OWN it. Tuck in the impostor syndrome and charge forward. Allow yourself to be celebrated, even among luminaries. You belong.

That is how I finally met Oprah, after being in many rooms with her over the years but never having the courage to introduce myself.

On three previous occasions, I actually said that when I finally met her, she'd have already heard and known my name. Well, this time she chose me to be in the room with her. And I was still shocked by it.

All of it is related, and when you aren't standing in your greatness and you're questioning the grace you find, it is impostor syndrome at work. How often do we let that lack of trust in our amazingness block our blessings?

Impostor syndrome is the cousin of fear. Both are boundless bastards.

Impostor syndrome is the feeling of wearing a mask and playing a role that you don't feel is real. It is present in those moments when you feel like you don't fit in or measure up. We think everyone else has it figured out and we're the only ones struggling. Well, I'm here to tell you WE DON'T HAVE STUFF FIGURED OUT. Even those of us who are in our thirties and forties and have homes and families and careers. We're still doing the trial-and-error thing. We still have impostor syndrome ourselves—you just can't tell.

I let impostor syndrome trick me into thinking there was no way Oprah could have picked me for that SuperSoul100 list. I let impostor syndrome tell me that I was not worthy of where I was being placed and the opportunity that was presented to me. But impostor syndrome lies.

How many times have we let impostor syndrome convince us that we should say NO to YES questions? How many times have we dropped the key to the door we should be opening because we didn't think we were ready? How many times has impostor syndrome told us not to write the book, not to try out for the team, not to apply for the internship? How many times have we let impostor syndrome keep us from doing what we're supposed to do?

We let the voices in our heads spin tales of inadequacy, and we believe them. We look in the mirror and wonder if anyone else realizes that we're just faking it. We let it convince us that we are not good enough.

Impostor syndrome tells us that we need to be perfect; otherwise we are failing. And that is a MAJOR lie. Perfection is the enemy of progress, and it does not exist. All it does is stress us out, have us overthinking everything, and make sure our anxiety levels are through the roof. If you're constantly striving for perfection, you'll be so afraid of failing that you won't create or finish that thing because you think it won't be good enough. So then you don't let it into the world. Then nobody gets the value of your work, because we never see it because you're too busy constantly trying to perfect it. Take the pressure off.

Impostor syndrome convinces us that what makes us different reduces our worth, when it is truly the opposite. As I said in chapter 2, our difference is often our superpower. As a professional speaker who has taken stages all over the world, I often find myself in rooms where I am the ONLY Black woman, and I happen to be the keynote. Instead of letting it other me, I use it to double down on how necessary my work and my voice are.

My Blackness, on those occasions, is an anchor for me. When I walk out of the room, those in it will not forget who I am. You might not remember Scott and Tim, but you're going to remember Luvvie, who came in her fedora, her red lip, and sometimes a crispy pair of Jordans or wing tips. I must remember that I'm not in there because anyone is doing me a favor. I am there because I bring value to any space I'm in. My opportunities are not from people taking pity on me but are a result of consistent hard work over a sustained period. To deny that fact is to betray myself and the work I've put in. Impostor syndrome be damned.

My job while in the room is to give value and then try to figure out how I can ensure I am not the ONLY next time. I must recognize my privilege and figure out how to use it so I can leave the door open behind me for someone who looks like me. Because the next time I'm in that room, I don't want to be the ONLY (Black person, woman, person with rhythm, etc.).

Why should I feel out of place? Because I'm not like everyone else in there? Sure. But I am not in any way less than they are. How did the other folks make it? It's not necessarily because they're smarter. It's not automatically that they know more than I do. It's not because they're more clever. It's that they found the cheat codes or knew somebody who knew somebody.

Impostor syndrome tells us that everyone else is better than us because they seem to be further ahead or to have their stuff together more than we do. It tells us that we deserve less because we are replaceable. Impostor syndrome will have us questioning what people say about us that's good. We will ignore the fact that they say we're smart, talented, and gifted. But the moment someone tells us something opposite, we take that on as fact. We will very quickly believe somebody's negative ideas about us but question five people telling us something positive.

What would happen if we actually took on the positive things people are saying about us, instead of taking in all the negative? Maybe impostor syndrome wouldn't have such a strong hold on us. Maybe we could use the logic of those numbers to boost us up when we think we aren't ready for a big moment presented to us, or ready to start that business or ask for that promotion.

It lies to us. Impostor syndrome is a liar, and too many of us have accepted its lies as truth. How do we fight it? How do we kick it out of our heads, or at least turn the volume down?

I remind myself that:

I am not the best. I don't have to be. I am enough. The idea of "best" is temporary. The person who wins a race won it once. The next race, they might no longer be the best. Are they at least in the top three? Did they beat their own time from the last race? We can reach for being the best, but thinking we've lost just because we didn't win is the quickest way to psych ourselves out.

I've worked my ass off. At minimum, that hard work has earned me a ticket in. Even if I am not the best, the fact that I KNOW that I work hard is enough to grant me admittance to that room. My grind got my foot in the door. I can at least give myself that.

Even if I happen to be in the room by accident and by no doing of my own, I AM IN THAT ROOM. It is no longer an accident. Once I'm in there, I am already worthy. How do I make it intentional and purposeful? What is my assignment while I'm breathing in that air? I take the opportunity to learn from the best. I walk away from that room inspired, with a resolve to be a superior version of myself. So next time I AM in the room, I feel at home in it.

I've ended up in spaces with the people I admire most, and each time, I question how I ended up there. EVERY SINGLE TIME. But after I reflect, I go back to some of those reminders. I worked hard for this. I don't have to be the best. I am enough. Since I am here, then it is no accident. I walk away knowing that I need to keep doing what got me in that room, and I need to keep doing it well.

Impostor syndrome does have some redeeming value. It keeps us humble. It keeps us curious. Doubt has purpose sometimes. If we don't think our work is good enough, we strive to do better and be better. Which then makes us greater because practice does just that. It turns us into lifelong climbers who DO end up belonging in any room we end up in, because we've continued to work at our craft.

The folks who are super confident in their abilities without any question are the ones who don't become better. They think they're so good that they just need to show up. They are the ones who don't grow, because they're too busy singing their own praises and patting their own backs without the compulsion of evolution. Like the person who never practices their instrument and comes into band sounding like a cat whose tail just got stepped on.

Practice makes you get better. People who are great at things have committed to something long term and done it repeatedly.

Do not let impostor syndrome keep you from celebrating yourself, taking up space, and owning your dopeness.

M y grandmother always celebrated herself. I still think about how she smiled with her whole face whenever she told us what she was up to or a new thing she'd done. She was earnest in her pride in herself without diminishing herself or others in the process. And she would not allow others to speak for her. I remember going to a doctor's appointment with her, and the doctor, seeing this older Nigerian woman, assumed she couldn't understand English. He turned to me and said, "What is her birthdate?" Grandma, not missing a beat and smiling widely, said, "Ask me. I was born July 31, 1931." And I sat there like, "WELP. You heard the lady."

I want to be like her. If arrogance is the worst thing about me, then I'll be really winning. If thinking highly of myself and being self-affirming is a fault, I want to be the walls of the Grand Canyon.

Speak of yourself and your work with exclamation points, not question marks. When someone asks you who you are and what you do, speak definitively. "I write." Not "Well, I kinda write, sometimes?" If you don't know, they don't know. We must honor ourselves in a world that doesn't want us to, and we will wait for nobody's permission.

And above all, do not question the grace.

SAY

We need to use our voices. In this section, I ask us to speak up about what we want and need, because our silence doesn't serve anyone. Being quiet about our lives, stories, problems, and lessons does us no favors. When we want to say something and our voice shakes, we should take that to spur us forward, because that is when it is most necessary. Let your voice tremble, but say it anyway.

"WE ALL NEED TO BE THE CHALLENGER, BUT EVERYONE IS WAITING ON SUPERMAN, WHEN THEY HAVE RED CAPES TOO."

—Luvvie Ajayi Jones

5

SPEAK THE TRUTH

**We fear rejection. We fear punishment.
We fear hurting feelings.**

 There are very few universal truths, but one of them is that humans are wired to yearn for belonging. Another is that rice is the elixir of life. (I'm not arguing. This is my book, so I do what I want. HA!) But really, we all want to exist in the comfort of acceptance from those around us.

Which is why telling the truth, which can disrupt the harmony of agreement in a room, can be scary.

But I'm of the same mind as Oprah, who said, "Speaking your truth is the most powerful tool we all have." Chances are, like her, you wanna become someone who is able to make change happen with your words. You wanna be bold in the face of fear, to speak up or do something difficult. You wanna be someone who elevates any room they're in with integrity.

That's EXACTLY what a professional troublemaker does, and it's why being one is important. Whether you've let fear block you from speaking up in the past or you've had a hard time using your voice consistently, it's not too late to develop the habit.

Power tools can be really useful, but also dangerous when used recklessly. Truth-telling is no different. That is why I'm writing this guide. I hope it gives you the exact guidance you need to wield your honesty sword carefully and confidently.

Shout-out to those of us with sharp tongues who know we can slice people left and right with our words. We, especially, gotta know how to not cause chaos with our mouths.

Challenging people or systems isn't easy, and it is an intentional decision folks make. It is truly scary.

When I turned thirty, I went skydiving because one of my friends asked me to go with him. When he asked, I said YES so quickly that I couldn't take it back. It was such a strong yes that even I was shocked. Being a woman of my word, I stuck to it. So we traveled to some out-of-the-way place in Long Island and signed all types of documents basically saying if we went *splat*, no one was liable. We got on the plane and went up 20,000 feet. I was strapped to the professional guy who was jumping with me, and as we were getting closer, he strapped me so tight that I was off my seat. My whole weight was on him, and that actually gave me comfort because I was like, "Well, now you have skin in the game because if I die, you die too. Great, let's do this."

That momentary piece of courage instantly disappeared when we were sitting at the edge of the plane and I was seeing the earth beneath me. I was like, "Oh, this is a bad idea. I've done some stupid things. This is one of them. Why am I doing this on purpose? I'm paying somebody to fall out of a perfectly good plane." Talk about first-world problems.

The moment when we fell out the plane, I actually forgot how to breathe for three seconds. It was like my body's reflexes were like, "Nope, nope, we're not good at this. No." Then my body was like, "Remember? Okay, do that using-your-lungs thing." I took a deep breath and the parachute popped open and we started floating in the sky as my jumper gave me an aerial tour of the New York area. It was stunning, and I was so glad I did this nutty thing!

When I want to say something that might feel uncomfortable or difficult or bigger than me, I go back to that time when I jumped out of the plane and lost my breath for three seconds. I think about how when I caught my breath and was able to look at the earth in wonderment, all I saw was beauty. It was the best thing I could have done. It felt right, even as it was still scary.

Even though I've had practice being the truth-teller and the challenger all my life, telling the truth feels scary each time. I say this because a lot of times people believe that being honest comes easy for challengers. They think, "Oh, you've been doing this for a while. You're used to it. You're fine." No, it's never really fine. You just get used to the practice of telling this truth in spite of the fact that it's scary.

If you think about those challengers, the people who constantly make other people uncomfortable with their truths, or who show up in the best way they can no matter what room they're in, and think, *I wish I could do that*, I'm here to say you can.

We can't take for granted the person who usually challenges, because it is not just one person's job—it is all of our jobs to use our voices to speak truth to power. We all need to be the challenger, but everyone is waiting on Superman, when they have red capes too.

There is a parable of responsibility that I love, about four members of a group: Everybody, Somebody, Anybody, and Nobody.

There was an important job to do, and Everybody was asked to do it.

Everybody was sure that Somebody would do it.

Anybody could have done it, but Nobody did it.

Somebody got angry because it was Everybody's job.

Everybody thought Anybody would do it.

But Nobody realized that Everybody wouldn't do it.

It ended up that Everybody blamed Somebody,

When Nobody did what Anybody could have done.

For girls, this strength in numbers is especially important because we're so often in spaces where we're constantly being inter-
rupted. Or somebody else will say the exact same thing we just said
and get credit for our idea. It's easy to ignore one, and it's hard to
ignore two. You can't erase three. Strength in troublemaking numbers is necessary! Let's be backup for each other!

Instead, many of us are too willing to be quiet when it's needed,
and then we dole out empty microappreciations. If after the class
or situation, you walked up to the challenger and said "OMG, I'm
so glad you said that!" then you're trolling in microappreciation.
You're telling me when nobody's listening, and the currency I
needed is not even usable, and nobody's here to see it. If you cannot back me up in the actual situation, what is the point? Let's do

less of that and make sure that in the room, we're proverbially taking a stand, not waiting till it's all cleared out. Actually stand next to that person. Use your words to affirm people out loud to give them more credence.

Telling the truth is HARD. Consistent candor is not common, and that's because we are afraid of so many things about truth-telling. Let's go through them:

FEAR OF REJECTION

You might have a friend, crush, or family member you need to say something to, but you're scared to damage the relationship. You're worried that your vulnerability might turn into you losing a valued member of your life village. You're afraid they'll walk away from you because people do not like to be challenged or opposed. And oftentimes, if we're having tough conversations with them, it's because we want them to atone for something they've done or to adjust a habit they have. Shout-out to those of us with abandonment issues. (It's me. I am "those of us.")

There are three things you should consider if you're struggling with a fear of rejection:

1. Your feelings are valid. You feel how you feel, and that's just how it is. I sometimes try to convince myself that my feelings aren't hurt because I don't wanna have to have the tough conversation. It would be easier if I was just FINE with what was said or done to me. But that never works, because you cannot logic away heart hurt. At best, you can swallow it down and compartmentalize, or even repress. But your feelings are still there, in the emotional fetal position. Meanwhile, this person has no clue you're trapped in a glass case of negative emotions, spurred on by them. Which is why . . .

B. Not telling them is not a great option, because your silence can become resentment. You're sulking somewhere, angry and hurt, while the other person is living their best life, oblivious to the pain they've caused you. All it does is allow this feeling to fester. Who wins? NOBODY. Not you, because your spirit is bothered. And not them, because they don't know the truth of what they broke, and therefore they cannot fix it. Resentment is poisonous.

iii. You owe them a chance to fix it. Getting the courage to speak up to a loved one is a gift because you are giving them the chance to show up for you when they disappointed you previously. We are all flawed, and even when we try our best, we will fall short. We will unknowingly do something that hurts someone we love. But when we are faced with the silent treatment as a result of us being HUMAN, we are being punished without due process.

And if they double down on their foolishness, showing that they knowingly hurt you . . . well, then you know something that lets you make a decision. "Is this person treating me with care? Should I give them continued access to me?" Quickly, your fear of rejection might turn into you deciding to be the one who rejects a friend, partner, or kinfolk who is not good for your spirit. If they reject your truth or are callous about your feelings, maybe they aren't your people.

The truth will get you the answer you need either way. If someone cuts you off because you voiced a thoughtful truth, it's more about them than you. And it hurts like hell to think about losing someone you care about, but some goodbyes are necessary. Grieve what you had and let them go (easier said than done, but, ultimately, you will have to do it).

FEAR OF PUNISHMENT

When it comes to telling the truth or speaking up, punishment is a real and acute fear. What if we face retaliation (emotional, physical, financial)? The world, after all, is full of petty and vindictive people. You might have a teacher or advisor who makes school difficult for you and others, and you're afraid of what could happen if you speak up. You might hear "NO," and that itself feels like punishment, even though most NOs won't kill you. If the person wields power over you, punishment is possible when we use our voices, so I absolutely understand this.

But here's the thing: What if that punishment never comes? What if we stop ourselves from doing or saying what's right and what could change things for the better because we are afraid of a phantom consequence that won't happen? We'll talk about these possibilities (in detail) shortly.

FEAR OF HURTING FEELINGS

Maybe you aren't afraid you'll be cut off or punished, but you hate the idea of hurting the feelings of someone you care about. Your intentions are good, you love them deeply, and being the catalyst for their pain gives you a stomachache. I get it.

The things to consider about the fear of rejection are the same things to consider here. But also keep in mind that you're navigating a fear of discomfort too. We don't want the weird feelings that come with loving confrontations (an oxymoron, mayhaps?). But hurt feelings are temporary, and honestly, they are a requirement.

Hopefully, that friend or sibling or adult whose feelings are hurt sees it as a growth opportunity.

Above all, I want you to know that you are not responsible for other people's feelings. You are not the chaperone to other people's reactions, because all you control is YOU. How they take it is completely out of your hands. As a type-A control freak, this is something I still struggle with. It's tempting to wanna supervise someone else's emotions, but it is truly an exhausting mission that often fails. Save yourself from the headache.

FEAR OF GETTING IT WRONG

You don't wanna get it wrong—either the situation or how you deliver the message. You don't wanna be judged, humiliated, or misunderstood. Those fears might keep you from speaking up. Understood and duly noted.

But here's what I want you to know: there is no REAL "getting it right," because anyone can take anything from what you said. Even the RIGHT tone can upset someone.

Take the pressure off yourself. Your delivery doesn't have to be perfect. Give yourself permission to be imperfect upfront and to use vulnerability in the moment of truth. And if you're afraid of getting it wrong, SAY THAT out loud. The truth is sincerity, after all. That includes you being honest about the discomfort of your moment of courage. For example: "Hey, it's kinda tough for me to say this." Or "Okay, so I'm a little nervous, but I'll say this anyway." This candor shows you're human, humble, and tuned in to the fact that what you have to say has you on high alert. But also note that your discomfort does not invalidate your feelings. Your fear does not nullify the point. And in the right room, in front of the right people, it will probably be received with the heart you intended.

It's okay to get it wrong too, because if you decide later on that you didn't like the words you used, or your tone, you can once again choose honesty and tell the person, "I messed up. I'm sorry." An apology is always on the table. Integrity is always worthy.

FEAR OF BAD TIMING

Is there a perfect time to drop truth bombs on folks? In the past, you might have wanted to speak up but stayed silent because you weren't sure if it was the anointed and appointed time for your voice to rise above the wackness. And then, afterward, maybe you thought about it some more and kicked yourself because you felt like you missed the right time.

Well, let me say that the truth can be early, but it ain't never too late. The truth might drag its feet, but when it shows up, we're all better for it. If you missed what you thought was the right time, you can return to the person like, "Hey, that conversation we had the other day? I gave it more thought and I wanna revisit it." Or "I know I didn't say anything last week, but it's been on my mind and I wanted to circle back with you."

We have to give ourselves permission to mess up. Humaning is hard, and our constant need to GET IT RIGHT gets us stuck. Our pressure to have it together actually makes us fall apart in more ways than we realize.

And I know you're wondering, "Is there a time NOT to speak up? Is there a way I can know that now's the time to ZIP IT UP and be quiet?"

There are three specific times you can clam up:

> A. You are flooded and overwhelmed. Something was said or done that has you feeling so emotional that your thoughts are cloudy and your impulses (not logic) take over. When I get especially angry, or hurt, I might start to cry. The tears aren't because I'm sad, but it's like my feelings have balled up, rammed themselves behind my eyeballs, and then poured out in water form.
>
> In those moments, the TRUTH should take a back seat because I am liable to lack EVERY FILTER and lose

my whole sensible shit. Which serves no one and is not productive for anybody. These are the times when fifteen seconds of words can destroy ten years of friendship. In those times, I just gotta STFU and feel my big feelings instead of opening my mouth and throwing word grenades.

You can still be honest, though, and say, "I am angry. I would rather not speak right now."

Let the truth wait for when you are back in control of your body and your words.

2. You are on the receiving end of a loving critique. Someone you love is telling you about something you have done or said that rubbed them the wrong way. They might be a friend or someone you're thinking about partnering with. Now, there are two sides to every story, and what might be happening might not even really be your fault. Or it might be a projection of their crap. I know, girl; it's happened to me too. But your job at that point is to LISTEN. This ain't the time to tell them that they're raggedy too. That's the TRUTH, but when used in that exact second, it is defensiveness. If you throw their truth back at them to make yourself the hero, you're indicating to the other person that they can't be emotionally safe with you. Instead, tell them, "I hear you.

Let me reflect on this and get back to you. But I am listening."

And then come back and make your case. Maybe in telling them you missed their birthday party because you were actually upset at how inconsiderate they've been, you'll realize "Aw, shit. I should have been honest with them first." We are all walking around scared and creating cycles of resentment that could have been handled if we made the choice to be courageous.

However, there is definitely a time to tell truth to go to hell, and that is if:

iii. You will be in danger. If what you have to say will lead to your physical harm, please choose silence to avoid violence. Protect yourself at all costs because your survival is of the utmost importance. I will never advocate for you to use your voice if it will lead to harm upon your body or destruction of your basic needs. Sometimes, the truth can antagonize people, and if that person is Satan's mentee, it won't go well.

I think about how girls and women often have to be quiet when WE are antagonized, purely for our physical safety. Like when we're walking down the street and get catcalled. How many of us have been followed when we speak the basic truth of "I don't want to give you my number?" How many of us have had to LIE and say "I have a boyfriend" just for the guy to back off? How many times have we had to give our number because we fear that if we don't, we could be assaulted? How many people have done all of that and have STILL been abused, attacked, or even killed?

We do what we must to stay alive in this landmine of a world, and sometimes, that means we know the time isn't right to say something. Sometimes that means we have to outright lie.

These aren't the only three scenarios we can choose to be quiet, but they are three that are good times to exercise the STFU coupon code of truth.

Fear is real. And using your voice in challenging moments is rife with anxiety and doubt. We're afraid to rock the boat. We're afraid to disrupt harmony. We're afraid of distancing ourselves from others. We are afraid of the power we wield with the truth. We're afraid of being the troublemaker.

In the absence of fear, there can be no courage. Because if

something is easy, it's probably not brave. If it were easy, everyone would do it. It is a choice to be outspoken when silence would be more comfortable, and that is brave. Truth-telling is not a universal habit, and I want us to choose courage more often. To help in this valiant quest, I present my Step-by-Step Guide to Truth-Telling. What do you do in the moment, in the meeting, at the dinner table? How can thoughtful honesty unfold in a room? What do you do when you are afraid of what could come from it? Let's get into it.

> THE WAY TO RIGHT WRONGS IS TO TURN
> THE LIGHT OF TRUTH UPON THEM.
>
> —IDA B. WELLS

STEP 1: ASSESS THE SITUATION

Someone said or did something and shifted the space and the energy of the room. Something ain't right, and you know it. You feel it!

Start by identifying what went wrong. What about the situation is off?

Was it a classmate's bad idea for the group project? Was it a racist joke that your uncle just made at the dinner table? Was it an unkind and underhanded statement your friend made?

What about this situation didn't sit well with you?

STEP 2: ACKNOWLEDGE THE FEAR TO YOURSELF

You want to take action and not let this moment pass, but you're afraid. Well, good. Fear is a red flag that something isn't right and you are now out of your comfort zone. It's also a sign that you're human.

Acknowledge the fear that's popping up to yourself. Name it and claim it. Which of the fears I identified earlier is it? Is it a fear of REJECTION or PUNISHMENT or HURTING FEELINGS or GETTING IT WRONG or BAD TIMING?

When you think about taking action and about being honest in this situation, what scares you most?

STEP 3: PRIORITIZE THE BEST-CASE SCENARIO

We are anxious about speaking up because we are afraid of the negative consequences that may follow. This is often when that FEAR OF PUNISHMENT takes over. We are afraid of failing or being punished or being rejected. And those fears can keep us tight-lipped—not once, not twice, but throughout our lives—until we realize one day that we no longer know HOW to use our voices to speak up during tough times.

Truth-telling is a muscle. But we've spent years fearing the worst-case scenarios that could come with authenticity, and in the process, that muscle has atrophied. I understand. Now I want you to face this fear head-on, consider what is actually likely, and weigh your options more.

Take quick stock of what the possible consequences for speaking up are, and make sure to include the best-case scenarios, not only the worst-case scenarios.

I recognize this is a new way of thinking for a lot of us.

We're so afraid of what could go wrong that we rarely imagine what could happen if it actually goes right. We'll sit in class afraid to thoughtfully challenge our teacher, afraid that we'll get suspended. We'll shut up, as if challenging our cousin's bad joke means we'll be excommunicated from the family. We'll remain silent as our friend disrespects someone else, afraid that our objections will mean we lose good faith with all our friends. We build our fears up to become dragons in our heads and then allow those dragons to stop us from getting to the other side.

We're so worried about what could go wrong, we've eliminated the possibility of our best-case scenario happening. We're choosing the NO automatically when the YES could be game-changing.

Instead of eliminating the best-case scenario, prioritize it.

When confronted with a truth-telling situation, get really real with yourself. You might go through this process quickly in your head in the moment or you might wanna think through and write it down over a few minutes or days (or, if super serious, even a month). I've done that.

Ask yourself:

What is the best-case scenario? What is the worst-case scenario?

What could go right? What could go wrong?

What if they tell me YES? What happens if the answer is NO?

What does SUCCESS look like in this case? What does FAILURE look like?

Let's look at how these questions play out with a specific scenario: You want to have a conversation with a friend about how they've been treating you, and how it's hurt your feelings. But you're afraid to have this friend reject you and your relationship. So you don't know what to do.

In that case, getting real with yourself and examining all the possible scenarios might look like:

BEST-CASE SCENARIO	WORST-CASE SCENARIO
• What is the best-case scenario? • What could go right? • What if the answer is "YES, you're right?" • What does SUCCESS look like?	• What is the worst-case scenario? • What could go wrong? • What if the answer is "NO, I reject it and you?" • What does FAILURE look like?
Best case: Friend says, "YES, you have great points. I am sorry I treated you that way. Thank you for telling me, because I want to make sure I don't do that to anyone else." Makes you feel more appreciated, less stressed, and more supported. **AMAZING best case:** Friend apologizes, promises to make it up to you, and sticks to their word. The whole situation brings you both closer together and shows you that you can show up as yourselves, even flawed, and still have a safe space.	**Worst case:** Friend says, "NO, you're wrong. I don't know what you're talking about," and doesn't listen to you at all. Your feelings are really hurt, but you know more about this friend now. You can determine how much access they can have to you in the future. **Apocalyptic worst case:** Friend says "NO, you're wrong, and I don't want to be friends anymore." And your honesty is the reason this friend cuts off your relationship. You are heartbroken about this loss, and everything sucks.

Read this and reflect on what's actually at stake. Assess the reality of the situation and act, knowing you are clear on what could actually happen if you use your voice.

Sure, that apocalyptic worst case is scary. But there's one thing we should ask ourselves when we're afraid of the hellish worst-case scenario: Is it LIKELY to happen? Like . . . of all scenarios, is that one the most possible? Many times, the answer is NO. A lot of things would need to go wrong for you to lose a friend simply for telling them they hurt your feelings. And remember, it takes two for a friendship to end. If it does, after you've approached them thoughtfully, you have done your part.

Next, ask yourself: Is my survival and the survival of others at stake?

Many of us are sitting in ivory towers, where the fear of punishment in our heads is overstated. I think about Black and Brown people whose voices and courage have caused them to be hurt or incarcerated or even killed. They aren't sitting in a cushy meeting on Zoom, afraid of not being invited to the next hangout. They are on the front lines, telling the truth about racism, white supremacy, queerphobia, and more. They're laying their lives on the line because the best-case scenario of using their voice and work is that systems of oppression are overhauled to no longer marginalize people based on how much melanin is in their skin, who they worship, or who they love. Their best-case scenario is transformative change in our world, while their worst-case scenario is losing their livelihoods AND their actual lives.

Yet they persist. They have weighed all these things, and even though they are often placed in real danger (physical or otherwise), they move forward anyway. THIS is true courage. The rest of us might not be called to do that work, but we can at least put our fears into perspective.

Run through the scenarios exercise and you'll often find that you might have added a bit of color to what could happen as a result of you using your voice. You have invited that dragon you created to sit on your couch and have tea.

If you decide to move ahead and take action, there might be consequences, yes. But by choosing not to take action and instead choosing to stay where you are, you're actually choosing failure in advance.

If the worst-case scenario is likely AND would put you in danger, by all means SAVE YOURSELF.

If it's likely, but there is no real danger to you, ask yourself: What is keeping me quiet? Can I deal with whatever that scenario is?

If the worst-case scenario is NOT likely, then the stakes are probably not that high.

Move forward with speaking up now, knowing that you are prioritizing the best-case scenario for the betterment of the room.

STEP 4: ASK THEM A QUESTION

Now that you know you're going to challenge this thing, start by developing a deeper understanding of the situation. This accomplishes two things: It affirms or denies your interpretation of the event, giving you that deeper understanding. And it allows the other person to reflect, which can lead to a change of heart OR a double down. Both are useful.

When you ask a question, the person has to dig deeper into their own words, thoughts, and actions. And if the person repeats their wrong (be it a wrong idea, wrong belief, or wrong action), then you can govern yourself accordingly. Questions are also a really great way of challenging people. This is what happens in therapy. Your therapist is really asking you a whole bunch of questions, without telling you much, letting you lead yourself to the solution.

If what happened was an insensitive joke or comment, ask the person, "Can you explain it to me?" Either your curiosity will have them explaining their crassness or, hopefully, they will stop in their tracks, apologizing because they recognize how out of line they were. If they gleefully explain it, well, now you have information you can do a lot with.

Asking a question also buys you time as you gather your thoughts and further process what just happened.

PERSON: HA! You know how those people's food smells terrible?

YOU: *straight face* You mean Nigerians? How do their food smell?

What you just established there is the fact that you are willing and ready to challenge foolishness in your midst. It tells the other person that you aren't willing to brush off tactlessness, and they can find themselves in holes they dug.

STEP 5: ASK YOURSELF THE THREE QUESTIONS

When you've taken the time to zoom out and assess the situation you find yourself in and then considered the consequences—weighing the best-case and worst-case scenarios—you're almost ready to speak the truth in hard situations.

When it's time to say the hard things, I ask myself these three questions to check in with myself:

Do you mean it?—Is this thing something I believe?

Can you defend it?—Being the challenger, I also have to be okay with being questioned and prodded. My ideas need to be explored deeper. Can I stand in it and justify it? Do I have receipts?

Can you say it with love or thoughtfully?—Is my intention good here? I might think I am righteous in my indignation or in my questioning, but am I saying it thoughtfully and with love? No matter how righteous it feels, no matter how true it might feel, if I say this thing in a way that's hateful or makes people feel demeaned or less than, the message will not land.

Do I mean it? Can I defend it? Can I say it with love? If the answer is yes to all three, I say it and let the chips fall. Whether I need to present a challenge in a meeting or to a friend or to my mom, I run this checklist to keep myself from being completely tactless. It holds me accountable to what I'm really saying and keeps me in check with myself.

Telling people around you thoughtful truths is a form of love. It says, "I care enough to hold you accountable. I care enough to move past my comfort zone to meet you and watch your back." It says, "I want you to win, so here I am, doing my best to support you with consideration."

This checkpoint does not guarantee people will receive your message. It's not a foolproof method, and there are still times I make mistakes or say something I shouldn't. But these questions help you keep your intentions good. Mind you, good intentions might still make for bad impact, but they give you a place to start. Be as thoughtful as you can be. How the challenge lands isn't in your control. Once you have thought about it, you're not being impulsive, you're not being hateful, you're being your solid self, you've done your best. Your job is to honor yourself and be the person who makes you proud at the end of every day.

STEP 6: SLAY THE DRAGON— SAY IT THE BEST WAY YOU KNOW HOW

Soooo you're ready to say this thing. It's time to slay the fear dragon you created (one that's probably bigger than the actual issue in front of you).

Say the thing that is difficult even though you might be uncomfortable when you do. Depending on who's in front of you, you can even admit that part: "This is really hard for me to say, but I think it's important." "I don't like tough conversations, but this one feels necessary." "I feel like I'm going against the group, but I want to honor myself here."

Be proud you did it scared. Take a deep breath. Chin high. I'm really proud of you. Keep doing it SCARED.

STEP 7: DO IT ALL AGAIN

There will be countless opportunities for us to speak truth, use our voices, and slay fear dragons. If you missed the chance last time, don't beat yourself up. Just commit to doing better next time, because there will always be a next time.

Relationships can reach a deeper understanding after tough conversations. Friendships can become more meaningful. You might prove your leadership qualities at your job and save your company from public embarrassment.

Similarly, relationships can break up after being challenged. Friendships can end. Jobs can be lost.

Telling the truth doesn't come with guarantees. It doesn't always make you the HERO. History is littered with disrespected truth-tellers who we later revere because hindsight is 20/20.

But history was also built by the troublemakers who insisted on doing this hard thing for the greater good over and over again. The world we live in exists, as good as it is, because of the disruptors who constantly slayed dragons even though they didn't know what would meet them afterward.

To honor ourselves more, we need to rise up to the challenge of questioning those we know, love, or care about. The ones in our community (professionally and personally) are the ones we can reach. When we are at the table, let's not walk away lamenting what we could have done or said. Let's walk away knowing "Well, I did my part." If my silence will not make me proud, and if my inaction will convict me, I know that I have to tell the thoughtful truth. Because ultimately, the judge that matters most is me.

Courage is a habit. There isn't a truth-teller gene or personality trait. It is a choice that people make day in and day out to show up, to be uncomfortable, and to use their words with integrity. You can start making that choice now and the next time you are presented with the option. And then do it again. And do it again. VOILÀ! You too are a truth-teller. It's a commitment to yourself, to those around you, and to the world that you will be the person who uses their words to make the spaces they're in better.

I say this as a Black woman who is constantly speaking truth to power, who is trying to do it in the most real way she knows how, who sometimes missteps: the greater version of ourselves is the version that is willing to be courageous in the very toughest moments. Because those are typically when we need to be most courageous. When it's that scary, when you want to go hide under a blanket, when somebody is telling you you should be more quiet, do not be more quiet. If you're compelled to do or say this thing, then you're probably supposed to do or say it.

We need to prioritize the truth, because the world is full of things to point out, injustices to fight, systems to dismantle. If we're not starting with honesty, how do we know the problems we need to tackle? You can't fix something you don't know is broken.

You don't lie your way to an equitable world or coddle your way to equity. We gotta find our individual integrity and our collective candor for the greater good, and we start by being honest, in whatever space we're in.

No one said this would be easy, but the things worth doing are usually not easy. You knew that, though. Truth-telling is a muscle, and like all muscles, it needs practice and exercise to be built. I hate working out, and anyone who says it's fun is a liar and a cheat. Yet I do it, because if I don't, it is to my own detriment. I will suffer most for it. Being a gatekeeper of truth takes practice.

Slay the dragon, friends. Tell the truth, even when your voice shakes. Tell the truth, even when it might rock the boat. Tell the truth, even when there might be consequences. Because that, in itself, makes you more courageous than most people in the world.

Use the three questions. Know your voice is necessary, and keep taking courage. Speak truth to power.

"WHAT ARE THE WORDS YOU DO NOT YET HAVE?
WHAT DO YOU NEED TO SAY?
WHAT ARE THE TYRANNIES YOU SWALLOW
DAY BY DAY AND ATTEMPT TO MAKE YOUR OWN,
UNTIL YOU WILL SICKEN AND DIE OF THEM,
STILL IN SILENCE?"
—AUDRE LORDE

6

FAIL LOUDLY

We fear being embarrassed.

 Failing sucks. No one wants to be humiliated. We are afraid that people will see us make mistakes and use them as ammunition to attack us. We are afraid we will say the wrong thing or do the wrong thing, falling flat on our faces, so to protect ourselves, we say and do nothing of note.

If you want to live an interesting life, full of color and impact, you will make mistakes. You will mess up. You will have moments that you look back on and go, "What the hell was I thinking?" And that's okay. Failure is necessary and essential for us to live loudly. But it is painful, it is usually unexpected, and it can knock us on our asses.

I have made a lot of mistakes, and I have failed out loud. It is a rite of passage for our greater good, and we must learn and grow from it.

Now, lemme tell you about my biggest public fail.

In 2018, on the day Aretha Franklin died and we all collectively mourned her, the conversation online turned to who would do her tribute. What artists could live up to Ms. Franklin's legacy to memorialize her in song? Names were being thrown around, and someone suggested the name of a beloved R&B artist who was big in the early 1990s.

In my occasional impulsiveness, having not heard the person's name in a long time or noticed them release any new music in at least fifteen years, I tweeted, "Under what rock did they pull that name from?" A few people were like, "That's actually a good suggestion." A lot more people were like, "Yeah, I wouldn't have thought of them first in this tribute lineup." The conversation continued as more names were thrown in the pot.

All was well. Or so I thought.

I woke up the next morning to my Twitter replies being in utter shambles. The conversation had shifted to the fact that since I was not born in the United States, and therefore not African American, I should sit out the conversation.

Thus started the biggest public fail I've ever had.

My friends started hitting me up as they began seeing it all over their own timelines, and I asked them for advice. Should I reply to this? Should I let it ride? Should I speak up for myself? Should I act like I don't see it and tweet other random things?

I chose the "sit this out" route for hours until someone tweeted something that I felt was derogatory about me. That's when my ego took charge and I replied. I responded by saying something about how I noticed that they were trying to other me. I also threw in something about them being so pressed by what I considered to be a simple tweet inquiring about how someone pulled up that particular musician's name.

That was me throwing gasoline on the fire, which caused it to now rage.

And rage it did. My name ended up trending on Twitter! *faints* I was the number-eight most tweeted-about subject in all of the United States for about an hour. Half the people were calling me everything but a child of God, and the other half were wondering why this word *Luvvie* was all up in their timeline. The one who was usually doing the judging was being judged. And very, very loudly.

I logged off. I knew it was bad because I kept getting texts from people checking in on me. "You good? I see what's happening. I'm sorry. Lemme know if you need me."

People were saying I was an entitled Nigerian who didn't know what the hell she was talking about. Folks dug deeper into my tweets, looking for ways to show that I was anti-American and anti–Black American or anything else that could be deemed offensive. Think pieces were written about me, and my name was plastered everywhere, it felt like. Anything I'd ever said about being Black in America was up for scrutiny. I was dragged.

I felt beat up on and lied about. So I wrote a response in a blog post, explaining myself and talking about how much I was not the person I was accused of being. Long story short, I didn't approach it well, because nowhere in it did I say sorry.

That blog post started a fresh firestorm, with some people becoming deeply invested in my fail and fall. One person went on Facebook and posted a status about me, saying, "I want to destroy her career." Someone made an anonymous email account where they sent anyone who was a brand partner or had booked me for an upcoming speaking engagement a message suggesting that clients disassociate from me. One popular anti-Black misogynist sent his audience to target me, bringing a lot of "go back to Africa" and "bitch die" comments onto my platform.

I was in shambles! I was NOT okay. Whatever tough skin or self-assurance I thought I had? This pierced straight through it. I felt like I was standing on a stage and someone had run up and stripped me of my clothes. I felt raw, naked, and unprotected.

But most of all, I beat myself up. I was on my couch crying and hating myself, a completely foreign concept to me. I couldn't eat. I refused to eat. My boo even took me to a crab boil, which is one of my faves, and I sat there staring at the delicious goodness of perfectly seasoned seafood and barely touched it. Just like how they say God gets mad if you pass by the color purple without acknowledging it, I bet God is pissed every time you waste a good crab boil. I lost eight pounds in a week. I, who am 120 pounds soaking wet on a gluttonous day when I drink a lot of water, lost eight pounds. So you know I was looking ghastly AF. It was not cute.

And it was my fault. I was beating myself up more than anyone else could. It's one thing to disappoint others. That sucks. But to disappoint myself was the tougher thing, because I felt shame in a way I never had before. I was so upset at myself because I made a mistake and said something I shouldn't have. I should have known better. I should have done better. I should have been better.

People went looking for things to be mad at me about, but it was MY fault for giving them things to find. It was my fault that they could say I'd been insensitive. Or said insensitive things. Or sometimes was just foolish. Had I not given them anything, they wouldn't have found anything to use to drag me through the mud.

I knew I was wrong. I wasn't a victim of people's meanness as much as I was a victim of my own big-ass mouth, which sometimes isn't as thoughtful as it should be. My two feet, which were always anchored to the floor, rooted in really liking who I was, felt shaky. I had faced backlash before, but not to this level, and not for this long. It felt unrelenting.

So I went dark online. My friends called me to check in and, at the worst moments, to remind me of who I really am. They gave me stern talking-tos in the middle of assurance, and they kept me from going deeper into the rabbit hole of shame. My partner said, "You let people steal your light."

I made an appointment with my therapist, because SOS! I was not okay! When I went in a few days later, she told me I was exhibiting symptoms of posttraumatic stress disorder (PTSD): disrupted sleep, lack of appetite, and an acute sense of being in danger even in mundane moments.

The incident had knocked me off my square in such a major way. I was drop-kicked off my game, and I ran away and hid. I was afraid I would never recover from this thing and my name was taking an irreparable hit. I legit wanted to quit everything and move to a small town somewhere and be a librarian. Because: dramatic.

The worst part? It made me afraid of my voice. I questioned my judgment. Up until then, I had walked through life rarely doubting my confidence in my voice, the biggest gift God had given me. But after facing this very public backlash, born from using my voice in a careless way, I began second-guessing my gift. I was scared of my own bold shadow: "If I say this thing, will people get mad?" I felt flutters in the pit of my stomach whenever I'd want to say something, truly afraid and taken right back to the moment when I saw my name on Twitter's trending list. I stopped writing. I stopped speaking up. I hid.

For a year, I didn't write anything on my website besides the TV recaps I was commissioned to write. On Twitter, I was extra cautious about posting anything too strong, because I was afraid to ruffle the wrong feathers and start trending again.

I justified not using my voice as "Well, maybe I need to evolve out of blogging. Maybe my work needs to look different."

I was still feeling bruised by the humiliation of it all, so I wanted to leave it behind. That was my ego talking. That was the failure talking. It was fear talking.

My book agent was asking me, "So, what's book two gonna be about?" I told her I was still thinking about it. What would I even write about? What did I have to say?

Almost a year to the date, another legendary death rocked the world: Toni Morrison. The writer who I quoted on page two of *I'm Judging You: The Do-Better Manual*: "If there's a book that you want to read, but it hasn't been written yet, you must write it." Ms. Toni told us that, and who was I not to listen? Her words had literally been life's instructions for me. She was the woman who made me too shy to call myself a writer because I felt like her words were too great for me to be in the same category with her.

But that woman had left this world, and her death convicted me. I'd never met her, but her permanent absence jolted my spirit awake. It wagged a finger at me because I was choosing to lie down instead of doing what I was put here to do.

I was reminded that writers and artists don't stop because

people critique them, no matter how harsh they think it is. They don't abandon their craft because they feel misunderstood or their feelings get hurt. They don't leave their purpose behind because they have loud detractors. They take the mistakes they made and let them spur them to make even better art. God said weapons would form. You do not let them prosper by letting them stop you from using your gift.

The first thing I wrote was a tribute to Ms. Toni and what she meant to me, as the favorite teacher I never met. After that, I got the idea for this book. I had spent a year afraid of myself, of my voice and my gift. I could no longer let fear dictate my life.

My journey is truly one of fighting fear constantly.

I'd failed very loudly, very publicly. But how could I use that for something greater? That sense of defeat was for the greater good of me, and the only way it would be for naught is if I didn't become a better version of me because of it. I asked myself: Why did it happen as it did? How do I move forward? What am I supposed to learn?

So many lessons.

When it comes to failing, we come up with stories about who we are because of it. That is where the shame came in for me. I felt like I got caught with my pants down and my ass all out in the open. I felt exposed and raw and thought everything I'd achieved was clearly a sham because it was about to get taken away. As people pointed out whatever old problematic thing they didn't like from my raving dumbass twenty-four-year-old self on Twitter, I felt embarrassed.

The lessons were plenty.

THE OLD ME WAS NECESSARY

With therapy, I began to realize that the girl from then was necessary because she became the woman from now. And I had to thank her for the work she did and the person she was, because she led me here. Then I had to thank the me now, in her thirties, who is more aware of herself, the strength of her voice, and the world. I couldn't be me without her, so my shame was not needed. I needed to give myself grace and forgive myself for my mistakes.

I had to be kind to that girl from then, the one who was afraid to call herself a writer because she didn't think she could measure up to the title. That girl could've never written this book, could've never confidently shown up in these rooms that I've been in and done her best work. The person who used to talk before she'd think could not be the person with the platform that I have now because I wouldn't use it as responsibly as I do now.

But that girl had to exist so I could write about her and her mistakes and the things she had to learn through the fire. Luvvie 1.0 had to be here so she could grow into Luvvie 3.0, who could write this book.

NONE OF US BELONG ON PEDESTALS

Pedestals are for statues, and none of us belong on them. Not one of us. We are flawed people whose jobs make us seem grander than we are. No matter how talented, creative, or smart people can be, we all have the tendency to be trash sometimes—it's human nature. I am not infallible or smarter than someone just because I have a large platform. Nah. I got kicked off my pedestal and I hope people don't put me back on it, because I don't deserve it. Leave me down here, because I can't live up to the standards folks project onto people they follow online. I will disappoint you. I will let you down. I will mess up. But I will hopefully never stop learning how to show up in the best way I know how. I will not stop growing. I will not stop holding myself accountable to who I say I am.

WHEN THESE MOMENTS OF RECKONING HAPPEN, WE NEED TO NOT WASTE THEM

Another lesson for me? The judge will be judged. I often challenge people to do better. This also means I will be challenged to do the same. I will be in the court of public opinion too, because I'm bound to make mistakes. What matters is how I handle it and move forward. That is what I will truly be judged on, and on that, I was held in contempt.

I should have apologized without defending or explaining myself. People want to feel seen and heard when we have done harm. I needed to atone, take accountability, and promise to show up differently next time. I did harm, and I should have copped to it early.

A proper apology woulda been something like:

Hey, everyone, today has been distressing, and to see my name in the lights in this way is something I am not proud of. I fucked up and I'm sorry. My words made people upset. My intention, whether good or not, doesn't matter, because we all know intention is not synonymous with impact. I should know better and should be better. I need to make sure that I am being even more thoughtful with how I show up in the world. I have a major platform, and with that comes higher expectations. I won't always meet them. In fact, I expect to fall short again. But at least I can aspire to be better than I am. I'm sorry.

That humility could have saved me a lot of trouble, because I was wrong. Not just because of what I said, but because of how I acted at being challenged. I should have taken the knee and moved forward.

After all this, it also became clear to me that my name was bigger than I'd realized. I'm not just some random Chicago girl by way of Nigeria, tweeting and cracking jokes with her friends. I am Brand Luvvie, with more than one million total followers on social media. I am representing Company Awe Luv. No matter how much I think of myself as some girl who started writing one day and cool things happened, I am at the helm of massive reach, and it is clear that my responsibilities are greater. My voice carries. My platform is large. I owe the best of me to an audience that's larger than ever before and bigger than I ever imagined. I have to act accordingly.

This doesn't mean I change my voice, but it does mean I have to move slightly differently. I used to be David but now I'm Goliath, and that's a tough pill to swallow. I'm no longer the underdog who can throw bones, but the big dog who gets bones thrown at me. That, for me, is frightening. It means who or what I speak about now has to be different, because my platform is larger.

The whole incident felt like God was grabbing my face and telling me, "You're at new levels. I need you to move different and be more responsible." I mean, did He/She/They have to make it so painful? Probably. My stubborn ass probably needed that jolt of reality. Message received, Holiness. I hear You, okay?

I was reminded I should always punch UP, not down. ("Punching up" is when you challenge someone with more power than you. "Punching down" is when you go at someone with less.) Yes, I need to punch up, and who that includes has shifted because I now wield more influence and weight. I can find myself punching down if I'm not cognizant of this dynamic and my stacking privilege. This is why humor is dynamic, and why comedians have to change their routines over the years. The legendary comedian who is doing $50 million Netflix specials can't do the same jokes he did when he was a struggling stand-up comic.

I also learned that I can be proud of my work, but I can't tie my worth to it, because it can be fleeting. While we should own our dopeness, we can't let all the outside praise we get go to our heads. People will love us one day and HATE us the next.

This experience made me more kind, because being at the end of hateful arrows feels harrowing. I've been scathing in the past in my critiques of others, and it was a necessary heart check to chill on that. Growing up looks like being kinder.

Being in the midst of that storm reminded me I need to help other Black girls and women when they find themselves in similar positions. To be a visible Black woman, especially, is to commit to being abused over and over again in hopes that it doesn't pierce your heart too much. I now make it a point to check in on the prominent ladies I know when it becomes their turn in the fire. Hearing from caring voices, even if they aren't super close to you, is helpful.

It also made me wanna vigorously defend Black girls who find themselves called out for mistakes, big or small. This platform and this voice ain't just for the comfortable times. If people come for me because I've defended someone, I'll deal. I am loved and valued. I deserve to be defended and protected even on my worst days, and so do others.

It takes a lot to be a prominent Black woman. I admire Beyoncé, Serena, and Oprah for more than their work. I deeply respect the grace they show under constant pressure. They're photographed when their expression could be translated to shady and they trend for days, as all types of people make up whole storybooks about their frame of mind. And they keep quiet through it. That is what I don't have yet and am trying to learn: the art of shutting the hell up even as people try to come for you.

One of my mistakes was responding at all to some of the people who were coming for me. I'm the person who usually tells my friends to chill when something similar happens to them. I didn't take my own advice, and it blew up spectacularly in my face. I fanned the flame. Yes, I felt hurt, but we ain't gotta attend every fight we're invited to. Next time, I need to ask, "What would Beyoncé do?" Sis wouldn't even act like she saw it. Instead, she'd be somewhere creating amazing art as people talk about her recklessly. It's why I had to start paying my Beyhive membership dues. That woman deserves us stanning.

MY PRAYERS NEED TO CHANGE

As I grow and my career grows, I need to say stronger prayers. There's nothing I can really do besides try to always be thoughtful and learn from my mistakes, but I can't say I will never make a mistake again. So if I make the next mistake, does that mean I am now going to be knocked off my square for the next year, because all these arrows decided to point at me?

I'm also going to pray to be fortified in the instances when people call me what I'm not, because it's not going to stop. I can say the sky is blue tomorrow and somebody might be offended by it. Right? If they choose to be offended by it, they will be offended by it.

I have to be fortified, because when the weapons form, may they not prosper. I can't not fulfill God's assignment for me just because some people don't like me. I need to learn and get fortified and pray that my armor is stronger than ever, that it gets stronger by the day, that my feet are more solid and planted than ever. I need to pray that as a leader, I'm showing what it looks like to fail and move past it.

I think of my grandmother, whose prayers I know cover me every single day. Those three-hour middle-of-the-night prayers gotta be responsible for some of my success, because I've made it here in spite of and because of myself.

I am a recovering asshole who will use every face-plant as a step stool to be better, smarter, tougher, kinder, and more gracious. I'm thankful for that D I got in chemistry. I'm so glad I got fired/laid off from my marketing job. And trending on Twitter for being reckless with my words was a blessing. Each time I fall on my face, it's a cosmic reboot and redirection that sets me on the path I'm actually supposed to be on. It is a recalibration of my life's GPS. Failure always gets me to higher ground.

I have nothing to regret cuz the falls are necessary for me to learn the things I do not know (and they are plenty). We can fall flat on our faces and rise up from the ashes of our old selves, better than before.

I sleep well at night because I'm at peace with myself and my soul. I wake up in the morning and look at myself in the mirror and really love the woman who looks back at me. She's flawed AF but knows without question that she is better than who she used to be. And she knows her mistakes do not define her; her lessons do.

Similarly, you are not your worst moment or worst mistake. You know who you are (go back to chapter 1. That exercise comes in handy when you're in the middle of firestorms). In the midst of your mistakes, it might feel like the world is collapsing or you won't ever recover. But everything, even your worst moments, is temporary. Humiliation is temporary. The acute pain is temporary.

Know that grace and accountability can coexist. Grace makes you forgive yourself for your mistakes, and accountability lets you know that you must remember the lesson learned and that those mistakes can't be frequent. It's a dance you must do.

Failure is life's greatest teacher, and the only way we truly fail is to learn nothing from the valleys we experience.

7

ASK FOR MORE

We fear disappointment.

 One of my favorite mantras, which I heard a long time ago and still hold dear, is "It's better to live a life of 'Oh well' than a life of 'What if?'" Many of us are living the what-if life because we do not know how to ask for what we want, what we need, and what we would like. We are constantly leaving things on the table that could be for us because we are afraid of the nos folks might tell us. We don't wanna deal with the blow that comes from putting ourselves out there and possibly getting rejected, so we end up being people who never ask.

I wonder what would happen if we were given the permission to constantly ASK FOR MORE, from life and the universe, from relationships, from friends and teammates. What might happen when we realize that NO won't kill us but YES could change our lives?

I love this sentiment by the brilliant Paulo Coelho, author of one of my fave books, *The Alchemist*: "The mere possibility of getting what we want fills the soul of the ordinary person with guilt. We look around at all those who have failed to get what they want and feel that we do not deserve to get what we want either. We forget about all the obstacles we overcame, all the suffering we endured, all the things we had to give up in order to get this far."

We don't know how to ASK for things because we don't want to be disappointed. Some of us became these people by necessity. Maybe we don't have friends to count on. Maybe no one ever provides for us, so we've had to figure out how to do it ourselves. Maybe the only person there for us is us. Maybe we've had to be this person because no one else has proven loyal, reliable, or stable enough to show up in the way we need. Or maybe we became this person because we had some painful experiences the times we did ask for something.

Whatever your reason is, it's valid and I don't blame you. As someone who has had more than a few "What the hell was that?" experiences related to me asking for help, I get it. I feel you. We go together like kettle and corn. That is why I'm here to tell you to ASK FOR MORE anyway.

It took me going to therapy to really understand that I was some-body, in all my boldness, who was afraid to ask for more. Lemme tell you how my therapist, who is a kind middle-aged Black woman (who could be anywhere from thirty-five to sixty-five, but I can't tell, because we tend to be ageless and our Black refuses to snap, crackle, or pop), told me about my whole life.

I like going to therapy because I enjoy paying someone to read me for filth. During certain sessions, I end up word-vomiting about feeling stressed out. I pride myself on being Team I Get Things Done no matter what, both professionally and personally, and I handle pressure well, but even Atlas shrugged after a while, didn't he?

One day, I was particularly stressed out about work plus home stuff, and my therapist said, "Have you asked your partner for help?"

ME: No, I got it handled. He got things going on too. This is mine to handle.

HER: Why? Don't you think he would want to help you as much as he can?

ME: He would. He's actually asked me what he can help with.

HER: Why don't you tell him to take some things off your plate?

ME: Well, I figured that because I said I got it, I want to stick to my word.

HER: I see why you're stressed out. Your husband sees it too and has asked to help, but you aren't letting him help. What do you think that does?

ME: Frustrate me because I need the help and frustrate him because he wants to . . . Oh, you just tried to get me with my own wisdom!

HER: *blank stare*

ME: You're right. I'm tripping.

HER: Do you not think you deserve to be helped?

And that is when my head blew off my neck. Do I not think I deserve to be helped? READ ME. DRAG ME. SLAYYY ME with that truth!

This is how we ended up exploring how I put boulders on my back while other people carry rocks because I would rather shoulder the burden. This is partly because I trust me more to handle it and partly because I don't think I deserve the help because I tell myself that others need help much more than me. Meanwhile, my back is breaking, all so I can feel like I'm helping others not break theirs.

Did I just read you your life? Yes, I did. Welcome to Club I Got It Even to My Own Detriment. Our meetings are every other Tuesday. Please bring snacks that won't cause heartburn, for us not-so-young folks.

Let me break ME down for you. I've always been the Responsible One, and I feel a deep sense of responsibility for myself, my path, and my actions. I don't want people to worry about me. The world is enough of an unpredictable junkyard. I have never wanted to give those I love or those who I am around another reason to be anxious, upset, or stressed out. If I were a superhero, I'd be Super-Independent. I don't need anything from anybody. I haven't even asked anyone, my mom included, for money since I was seventeen years old. And I've worn this as a badge of honor for a long time.

As the Responsible One, that same insistence on not being a burden on anyone also came with the self-imposed duty to make sure the people around me were doing okay. Since I was fine, I felt obligated to make sure they were too. This turned me into the Giver Who Never Asks, and that is a problem.

Shout-out to those of us who are GIVERS. We define ourselves by how much we give to others. Our benevolence as a core value is something we are very proud of. (Remember chapter 1? Yeah, Auntie Generous over here.) However, GIVERS are usually bad at being TAKERS, which is a liability.

There are so many people who will give you the shirts off their backs but don't know how to receive something as simple as a compliment without feeling like they have to hand it back somehow. I'm a recovering giver, meaning it used to be impossible for me to ask for help or receive gifts without feeling like I owed someone.

But get this. How can we allow people to fully show us love if we don't allow them to be generous to us? We love the feeling that we get when we're like, "Hey, I just did this thing for somebody." So, then, why don't we allow others to get the same feeling when they give something to us, whether it's a compliment, a gift, or their time?

When you are only handing out without receiving, you might be unknowingly leading with your ego. Maybe deep down, you love being thanked. Maybe subconsciously, it feeds your ego to always be Captain Here You Go. We love how good it feels to give. Generosity also helps us hide our vulnerability. Always handing out help but never asking for it is ensuring we aren't seen as weak. Or maybe we don't think we deserve moments of service ourselves. We might not want people to think we're taking advantage of them. We don't want to show up as somebody who needs somebody else. It's a problem because we are not being fully honest with ourselves and the people in our lives.

n times of frustration, I've complained about how I've ALWAYS done everything myself and this is why I don't need anyone to do anything for me. Meanwhile, I've gone to the ends of the earth for people, even when they didn't ask.

One day, my husband basically channeled my therapist and read the scrolls of my life to me. He said, "You being so open-handed seems to be a function of you not wanting to exert the same pain point on somebody else. I'm going to challenge you to stop saying how much you don't need from someone. I want you to stop saying how much you don't ask for things from people and how much you take care of everything yourself. You say it out loud so often. I ask that of you because what I hear when you say that is you're wearing it as a badge and accomplishment. If this was the Struggle Olympics, that may be okay, but it's not."

You should have seen the way my edges instantly retracted into my scalp. DID YOU JUST READ ME SO ACCURATELY WITH MY OWN WORDS? You know when someone says something that is so on point that you have no comeback because your brain is doing the "But They're Right" Running Man? That's what happened when he said that to me. The realization that I had come to define myself as someone who did not need anyone. What cookie did I think I was gonna get by running myself into the ground? What martyrdom did I think I was aiming for?

What is the win when we insist on being self-sufficient even in the moments of drowning, when all we need is a hand as we flail in water? Are you saying there's no Lived a Low-Maintenance Life and Needed No One cookie? Well, damb. I think about the Brené Brown quote "I've learned that gasping for air while volunteering to give others CPR is not heroic. It's suffocation by resentment." A WHOLE SERMON.

We, especially Black girls and women, are so used to being called strong that some of us consider it a weakness to need the support of the people we consider community. We cannot base who we are on how little help we need, or how much we are helpful to other people. Because what if there comes a time when we have nothing to GIVE? Does that render us terrible people? Do we lose our compass? Do we feel less than because of it?

When we don't ask, or we don't receive well, we might be blocking our blessings. This goes beyond the times we need help. When we do not know how to ask for what we need or ask for more, we end up receiving less than we should. The truth is people will give you the absolute minimum if you let them. Sometimes we aren't even "letting" them. We are afraid of being TOO difficult or demanding (hey, chapter 2), so we accept the first thing they offer us.

I come from a long line of hagglers, and my grandmother was definitely one. Haggling is an exercise in asking for more until you are satisfied. So why did I come to America and forget my haggling ancestry? I should have been treating job negotiation like a Nigerian market, where the motto is "Always ask for what you want." The first no isn't what they mean. Keep asking, and even if you don't get exactly what you want, you will be as close to it as you can get. "At least you tried" is a way of life.

When Mama Fáloyin would come to the United States, she'd ask me to take her to her favorite flea market in Chicago. By me taking her, she meant she needed me to come to be extra hands to hold the plethora of stuff she would be buying. Also, to push the second cart.

My freshman year of high school, K-Swiss shoes were all the rage. My mom, being the coolness blocker that she was (see also: single mother who couldn't afford to buy $75 shoes), wasn't getting me a pair. And since my allowance was like $5 a week, the save-up for them would take months.

So me and Grandma went to this large warehouse that honestly instantly overwhelmed me. I had insta-regret the moment we stepped in there because ten thousand square feet of disorganized bins of stuff you have to rummage through is my idea of hell on earth. (That and having to take a Spirit Airlines flight.) I was ready to drop all my sins for sainthood, because if real hell was this, I SURELY wasn't tryna go.

After about ninety minutes of rummage fest, I somehow stumbled upon a pair of all-white K-Swisses. They were mid-length, with the five stripes and the white laces. WHAT?!?!? Look at my luck and God! Those shoes were the apple of my eye instantly. (Teenage Luvvie was tacky, doe, so she didn't know them shoes were some UGLASS things and that is why they ended up in a bin in a random warehouse, not in a store on a shelf. All I knew was: OH SNAP! I CAN HAVE NAME-BRAND SHOES.) I didn't care that they basically looked like high-top socks with rubber at the bottom or that someone had done a bad job of gluing rubber under some dingy socks (because, mind you, they were white fabric, not even leather).

Grandma saw my excitement (cuz I was probably looking like Eeyore before this) and told me to put them in the cart. I was trying to not get my hopes up, because I knew they weren't gonna make it home with me. They were gonna be too expensive. I just KNEWED it. So we get up to the cashier and the shoes ring up as $25. I'm like, "Well, there goes that. She's gonna drop these." Instead, Grandma goes, "My friend. These are for my granddaughter. Please. Can I have them for ten?" I'm in my head thinking, *This lady is nuts*, while also silently mourning the shoes I almost had.

Y'all. When I tell you my grandma somehow got them to agree to sell these shoes to her for $8? WHAT VOODOO SHE DO? And they threw in a mug she saw by the register for free. I was like, "THIS IS ANOINTING." Just bold and manifesting clearances. Gahtdamb superwoman. Ask and you shall receive indeed. Ask boldly, believing the answer is already yes.

I wore those K-Swisses OUT! Those five stripes were probably down to two by the time I was done with them. But the audacity to ask. It was everything. Ask for what you want. The universe might surprise you and say YES.

L emme drop a quick scripture on you right quick. Matthew 7:7: "Ask and it will be given to you; seek and you will find; knock and the door will be opened to you."

What would happen if we had the boldness of an older Nigerian woman who believes she can get what she wants through kindness and that smile of hers? Mountains could move!

Do not force yourself to want less to appease other people. Do not dumb down your needs so you won't want to ask for more. You want what you want. Ask for it. A NO will not kill you.

Ask for more, because if the fear of disappointment stops you from going for what you want, then you are choosing failure in advance. It's a self-fulfilling prophecy. If we don't think that we should ask for the thing we want, whether it's a promotion from our boss or more acts of service from our partner or more attention from our friends, then we are opting for the NO instead of trying for a YES. If we get the NO, we are still in the same place as we were, losing nothing. But what if we got the YES, which would lead us closer to where we want to be?

When you choose to let fear keep you in your comfort zone,

you might think that you're avoiding disappointment when what you're really doing is choosing that path, because you will know that you aren't getting what you want and need. The NO will not kill you, but the YES could save you.

My life changed when I got the courage to ASK for what I want. The courage to ASK people to stop doing things I didn't like. The courage to ASK people I work with for what I thought I deserved. The courage to ASK my partner for what I needed to feel loved. The courage to ASK my friends for their shoulders when I needed to cry. The courage to ASK the universe/God for things I thought were far-fetched.

I know we've heard "Closed mouths don't get fed." It is cliché. But it is true. We close our mouths as people do things to disrespect us. We close our mouths because we do not think we are in the position to ask. We close our mouths because we're afraid of NO. When I learned to open my mouth, my life transformed.

I didn't get smarter or cuter or less loud or less quiet or more interesting. But I was no longer so afraid to be vulnerable and say when I needed help. I was no longer tied to the thing of "I'm the one people don't worry about." I humbled myself and realized that life is not about taking on more than we can stand so someone else can soar on our backs.

You know what happened when I started asking for more? Magic happened. By magic, I mean people gave me more. The love I hoped people felt from me came back infinitely. I felt stronger, knowing that in this world, I didn't walk alone. I felt more loved, because I gave people a chance to show up for me and to feel just as good as I did when I was leading by giving. And I felt more confident, because things I'd dreamed, and some things I never even fathomed, started happening for me.

8

GET YOUR MONEY

We fear being considered greedy.

 Money runs the world, unfortunately, and we treat it like a taboo topic to discuss. How are we so shy about the thing that often dictates the quality of our lives? Not having enough money is expensive, and being poor is costly.

The eight richest people in the world have as much combined wealth as half the human race. That is WILD. There are more than seven billion people on this third rock from the sun and less than TWO HANDS of people hold half the wealth. And all of those top eight billionaires are dudes. It is not because they are smarter than everyone else, and it surely ain't because they work harder than everyone else. It is because capitalism has favored them, and they've learned to make money through the work of others. They have no guilt attached to making buckets of money, and the systems prop them up to allow them to do so. They have no guilt for wanting to be financially prosperous.

Girls and women are discouraged from caring too much about money, because we're supposed to be constantly service-minded, even as others plot how to stack their coins. People assume we want to volunteer our time, giving our energy and skills without pay. Women do a lot of nonprofit work, and we make up 74% of people in that industry, which historically has low pay and long hours. In a capitalist society, philanthropy is a burden that we overwhelmingly bear, and that has real consequences. I want you to know that doing good in the world is important, but you do not have to personally suffer and sacrifice your well-being to give back.

We worry that if we care a lot about money or talk about it too much (levels that are super subjective), we are being greedy. Even though we HAVE to care about money to survive. Everything we get to do is tied to our financial wellness.

Here's why I want you to get comfortable talking about money. When I got out of college and started really living on my own, I realized how little I knew about what it took to be a functioning adult, because I never learned the lessons about it from my parents or from school. Sometimes, adults act like kids can't handle the information, even though they know that one day, those kids (you) will grow up to NEED THIS INFORMATION.

I'm asking you to double down on being a professional trouble-maker if you are already one. And I'm asking you to become one if you aren't already. In order to be able to make this good trouble, you need to be financially secure—it gives you a cushion so you never have to stay in a job that you hate, a relationship that doesn't serve you, or a situation you need to remove yourself from. Money isn't the key to happiness, but it does give you the freedom to make decisions without feeling caged.

So, I wanna tell you four things I wish someone would have told me about money when I was young to prepare me for adulthood.

SAVE YOUR MONEY EARLY AND OFTEN

One of the habits that you should start developing now is SAVING YOUR MONEY. As you earn money, or are given money for whatever, you want to start putting some of the money away instead of spending it all. Your savings, which is the pot of money you have collected, is important because it plans for the future and plans for the goals you have. It means that you have a reserve somewhere you can tap into.

Your savings can be for emergency purposes. OR it can be an intentional pile that goes toward something you really want (could be shoes, could be a gadget, could be a trip).

How you save your money is by constantly living below your

means. It means that just because you have $20 doesn't mean you spend all $20. You can spend $10 and save $10. Right now, you might be getting an allowance from your parents. Do you spend it all once you get it, or do you spend some and put some away? I hope it's the second one.

You get some birthday money? Well, try to save half of it. When your favorite aunt slides you a big bill, save the whole thing! You'll start seeing your money stack up, and it will make you feel good because you'll know you have more options, and that you can take action to get yourself what you want when you want.

Ask any adult and they'll tell you one of the things we hate most about being a grown-up is that we have to pay bills EVERY MONTH. Being a human costs money, and I hate that part so much, but here we are. A savings account is important to have so you have backup, in case you lose your job or some NEW bills pop up that you didn't expect.

I call my savings my FREEDOM FUND. The freedom of choice is powerful, and that's one of the first steps to having it.

GROW YOUR MONEY

When you start saving your money, you can leave it in a bank account. Soooo if you put like $1,000 in the account, it will pretty much stay $1,000. You lose nothing, technically. BUT your money should actually be growing, not just sitting there.

This is where INVESTING comes in. Simply put, investing is putting your money into something that you think will be worth more later. So, as that thing increases in value, so does your money. You can invest in stocks, bonds, or even real estate. To buy a stock is to buy a share (a piece of ownership) of a company. So, for example, I could buy a share of Facebook today, betting that in one year, that share will be worth more money. On average, the stock market gets you an 11 percent return every year.

Let's say you start investing with $1,000 that you've saved over years of birthday money, graduation money, allowances, chores. If you invested that money in the stock market and added $20 every month to it, in ten years, you could have almost $7,000. All because your money is growing itself.

I didn't learn of investing until I was in my twenties. That is when I realized the importance of making sure I wasn't just watching my money sit in a dormant savings account. I lost over ten years when I could have been growing my money, but you don't have to! You can start investing even with $100.

One thing to keep in mind: investing is a long-term commitment. Don't put the money you will need in three months for those shoes in a stock—you aren't giving it enough time to grow. So, if you will be needing to spend that money sometime soon, keep it in the savings account. But if you are committed to this lifelong habit of watching your money grow, invest it.

There are lots of books that go DEEP into this topic. But I wanna put this bug in your ear so you can start thinking about when you would want to start doing this, when to have the conversation with your parents, and how much you'd like to start with.

KEEP GOOD CREDIT

In the United States, adults get a report card on their ability to pay back what they borrow and their ability to pay bills. It's called your CREDIT SCORE. It's super important because lenders, banks, utility companies, etc., use it to determine whether they should do business with you. Your credit score and the history of the payments you've made are given to you in a credit report. That report tells so much of your business and is used to make many decisions about your financial integrity.

Your credit score will be between 300 (terrible) and 850 (excellent). The goal is to be as close to excellent as possible, and anything over 720 is considered really good! How your score increases is by you having lines of credit (credit card, loans, mortgage, etc.) and paying your bills on time every month. Every time the lender reports that you paid, your score goes up. If you have credit cards, you also want to keep the balance (amount on your cards) less than

20% of your total limit at any given time. Sooo let's say your credit card lets you borrow up to $1,000. You don't wanna spend more than $200.

People who are at the lower end of the credit score range have a hard time getting loans, buying homes, and getting credit cards. When you fall behind on bills, you will get a derogatory mark on your report, and if you miss payments enough times, you could be sent to collections, which drops your points considerably.

Good credit is prioritized, but the thing about the credit system, like so many things, is that it is inherently unjust. It penalizes people who are low income, perpetuating the cycle of poverty by punishing people for not being able to keep up with their bills when they already don't get paid enough. People usually don't miss payments because they want to but because they have no other choice because they have no money. There are people who cannot even save money because after their bills are paid, not only do they have no money left, they might fall into further debt. There are so many people who are struggling with bad credit due to all sorts of tragedies happening in their lives. Or simply due to systemic racism and economic oppression. A lot of those people are Black and Brown.

These and other reasons are why I have to say that even though this is a part of the systemic game we must play, I hope you know that your worthiness as a human being is never tied to your credit score. This ranking system, like many others, can make us feel small if it isn't the number we think is ideal. I want to say here that

YOU ARE NOT YOUR CREDIT SCORE. Life happens, jobs are lost, and there are many things that could pop up unexpectedly.

So . . . I'm saying KEEP good credit in mind as you are on your financial journey. College is when a lot of us start making bad credit decisions, because we're on our own for the first time. So we take out loans or open credit cards and spend it all. Then we look up after four years, not knowing where all that money went and riddled with mountains of debt we'll have to spend years getting out of. If you can avoid this, PLEASE DO. There's a whole generation of people before you whose first credit fail was signing up for a credit card just to get some free pizza and spending it without paying it back. There are grown-ups who are still paying for that decision twenty years later. I'm hoping this won't be you, cuz your Cantankerous Auntie from Afar (me) warned you in a way she wished she was warned.

PS: That savings account I want you to have? Well, it comes in handy in the moments you might be short on money for your bills. I'm just saying.

ASK FOR MORE MONEY (NEGOTIATE)

I was probably twenty-eight years old the first time I asked for more money than someone offered me, and it blew my mind (and made me a little angry) that NO ONE had ever told me that I was supposed to negotiate money I was offered. I had spent my whole life saying YES to what people wanted to give me, without pushing back or speaking up that I wanted more. And it had done me a major disservice.

The last time I worked full-time for someone else was as the marketing coordinator of a nonprofit. At the time, it was my dream job. I remember applying, crossing my fingers, and hoping I'd be so lucky to get an interview. Well, I got the interview and aced it. In September 2008, I received my offer: "Your starting salary will be $35,000." Dang, I'd hoped I could get $40,000, but who am I to be greedy?? I instantly replied back to the email that I accepted.

If you don't take anything else from this book, please absorb this: ALWAYS NEGOTIATE YOUR JOB OFFERS. It doesn't matter how good the offer is! Always ask for more. Couple of reasons:

> 1. Nobody is doing you a favor by hiring you. NOBODY. You are hired to do a job because you have the skill. They need you to do this thing.
> b. You are supposed to negotiate. In fact, when you don't negotiate, you are going against standard practice. It's part of the steps of the game of business. You have the right to ALWAYS ask for what you think you are worth. The answer is less your business (you can't control that), but the ASK itself is FULLY your business (you control that). DO IT ALL THE TIME.

iii. The first offer is not the best offer. As in, people always have more money than they first bring to you. The first number thrown at you is NEVER the highest number someone can pay you. They offer you $40,000 as your annual salary? Odds are that they have $45,000 in the budget for you. Ask for $7,000 more, and they might meet you in the middle. Too many of us opt out because we are afraid. Which leads me to:

4d. You asking for more money (or vacay time or benefits) does not mean they will take back the offer. Just because you say "I want more" doesn't mean they'll say "We don't want you anymore." I know it is a major anxiety we have—that if we negotiate, they will somehow be offended and take everything off the table. They are not doing you a favor by offering you a job: they need you too. When a job finds you, their perfect candidate, they don't want you to walk away. THEY NEED YOU. So remove the fear that you asking for more will mean you lose the job.

People who are marginalized (women, people of color, and others) especially haven't been told to negotiate. Meanwhile, the number that we accept in the beginning of our careers follows us. That $35,000 affected every other number I received from that point from that company. A 5% annual raise for $35,000 is $1,750. Sooo that brought me to $36,750 after a year. Imagine if I had negotiated to start at $40,000. 5% of that is $2,000, which would bring me to $42,000. The same position and same company could have gotten me over $5,000 MORE in one year if I simply asked. Not asking for more literally costs us money. It is expensive to be quiet sometimes, and this is one of those instances. We have to ask for more money.

You can start practicing your negotiation skills with your parents (don't tell them I told you). HA! If they offer $20 as your allowance, ask them if it could be $25. The worst they can say is NO, and you still get the original.

There are entire books on how to negotiate. Consider picking one of them up.

The world is not a meritocracy, and the systems we live within weren't built for us to succeed. Somehow, we do it anyway. All our lives, we have received the jacked-up message that we are less significant and more disposable, and we should yield for everyone else's convenience. So then we internalize it all and wire our mouths shut to protect ourselves.

I do not blame us one bit. The world really has done the job of convincing us that we are liabilities instead of assets, and it's utter bullshit. Some of the fight has been abused out of us, so we are getting deceived left and right, underpaid, overworked, and underappreciated.

The systems of oppression stacked against us devalue us and render us at their mercy. I am VERY clear on that. White men are the measuring stick of it all because they've created those systems and run them like the unfair well-oiled machine that they are.

It is why white women make 79 cents for every dollar Biff makes.

Latinas make 54 cents for every dollar Chad brings in.

Native American women make 58 cents for every dollar Trent gets.

Black women get 62 cents for every dollar Brock takes home.

Asian women make 90 cents for every dollar Logan secures.

We are systemically hustling backward, and it's not okay. The world is unfair to everyone who is not a straight Christian white dude. It is set up for their triumph, their comfort, their wealth-building. It is designed for the rest of us to be born poor, live poor, and die poor. It is also designed to gaslight us, by teaching us to be afraid of what happens when we want the piece of the pie that belongs to us but that they've hoarded.

I want us to know that we are not being greedy for asking for what we're worth. And we are not being greedy for wanting financial independence. We are certainly not being greedy for wanting to make more money in a really expensive world.

Learning how to earn money, save money, grow money is up to us. I look back at how little I knew until I was already out in the world on my own and wonder how much easier my life could have been had I been told what to look out for.

If you are someone who wants to create a nonprofit or a campaign with the intent of helping the world out, I want you to help yourself first. And then help the world. Put your mask on first and all that jazz. I preach the gospel of us leaving the world better than we found it, but we also have to be able to leave ourselves better for it, not worse. We've been told that our goodness in this world is directly tied to how much of ourselves we sacrifice for other people.

Earn money. Save money. Grow money. Because in your hands, rising troublemaker, I trust that the money will not only serve you but serve the world. In the hands of a disruptor for good, an abundance of money becomes a form of economic justice, put to work for all our betterment. The best people who become wealthy spend their financial privilege creating circles of giving. That, in turn, makes real impact on the world. It is time for us to make sure girls and women are not living in poverty but prosperity. So . . . get your money!

9

DRAW YOUR LINES

We fear alienating people.

 We have to teach people what we expect from them and how we want to be treated. If we do not, we'll constantly have people getting on our last nerves, and life is too short for side-eye-induced high blood pressure.

Boundaries are some of my favorite things to draw. I feel an obligation to let people know when they do something I don't like, because as the professional cantankerous auntie that I've been since I could talk, I am not the most patient person at times. That's because I have some firm lines I don't want people to cross, and when they do, it instantly grinds my gears. Since I have zero poker face, my annoyance is usually written all over it, because my face is basically a visual outside voice.

For me, drawing boundaries is a matter of social grace and a form of love. We must create and vocalize our boundaries, no matter how much it might be jarring to others.

Having boundaries and drawing our lines is not about playing keep-away with people, and it isn't about preventing people from getting close to us (well, sometimes physically it is). It is about establishing the standards and the treatment we expect and deserve. It is giving people a guide to how we want to be treated.

People often feel entitled to our lives, energy, time, space, and platforms. Usually, it's not from malice but from habit, and we aren't used to creating and enforcing borders. We touch, kiss, and move other people's bodies. We manage other people's time. We infringe upon other people's platforms. It is how we operate as a society. What's wild is MOST people are annoyed by someone crossing their boundaries.

So why are boundaries so hard to establish? Why do we have such a hard time telling people to stop that thing we don't like them doing when it comes to us? Because we don't want to make people uncomfortable. We fear disrupting harmony, hurting feelings, and seeming difficult.

As I'm moving through the world, of course I must consider other people (I'm not a sociopath). But like the flight attendants tell us as we post our last Facebook message before takeoff, we must put our oxygen masks on first before we help other people with theirs. I need to feel as comfortable and as assured as I can. I am not obligated to use my time, body, space, or energy in ways that don't suit me.

However, while everyone else isn't necessarily responsible for my comfort, they might be the reason for my discomfort. Lemme explain. When I walk into a room, the people in it do not have to make sure I'm feeling attended to or feeling perfectly at home. HOWEVER, if the folks in the room start throwing insults my way, then they are liable for my uneasiness. That being said, my boundaries are my responsibility to voice, because what happens when people don't realize I've drawn lines in invisible ink? They're not to blame if they don't know. We often get mad at someone crossing boundaries we didn't establish, but we have to ask ourselves how the person could have known to do better by us or to do something different.

Did we tell our friend to stop reaching into our bag of chips without asking or even cleaning their hands? Did we tell our sibling that coming into our room without knocking is an invasion of privacy? Did we tell our parents not to call us our embarrassing childhood nickname when they come to our games? DRAW YOUR LINES with whoever you need to.

Yes, there are some universal boundaries we should all honor, like that consent should come before sex. A person should be able to walk down the street butt-nekkid wearing nothing but socks and a smile, and no one should touch them unless they have a sign that says TOUCH ME FREELY. Even then, I might still ask.

Besides that, we can't assume much else of anyone. Do we realize how much we go through life letting people talk to us and treat us any kinda way and doing things to us that we don't like? What do we do about it? A lot of times, we roll our eyes. Or we deep-sigh. Or we hope they magically stop doing that thing we don't like. But people will bring trash to you if you are a willing receptacle.

We cannot assume everyone is operating from the same understanding. We don't operate from the same mind frame. This is why we have to be intentional about speaking our boundaries out loud. We gotta speak up about the things or space we need from people. That is our responsibility. Whether or not people honor it is theirs.

Personal, professional, emotional, and physical boundaries are all important. We think we can't afford to tell people our boundaries for fear of ostracizing them. But really, we cannot afford NOT to tell people our boundaries, because when we are silent, we betray ourselves. And we must betray ourselves less.

One of my grandmother's biggest boundaries was being spoken to in a loud voice in the middle of conflict. Here's the thing: Nigerians do not have an inside voice at all. Come around my family during the holidays and it sounds like a hundred people are in the room, even if it's only twenty. Yelling as we speak to each other is a love language. Even now, when we get on the phone, we act like 5G cell phone service is not a thing and that our phones are tin cans connected by string. We are SO LOUD. We use whatever the "unnecessarily loud" decibel measurement is. I remember when I used to make fun of my elders for doing it. Now I'm an elder and I do it.

Even with those cultural values, Mama Fáloyin did not suffer fools when it came to how she wanted to be respected at all times. Yes, you might yell her name in glee when you saw her or to hype her up (in church and anywhere else). But if she was talking to you sternly and you raised your voice? There was hell to pay. By hell, I mean dramatics.

GRANDMA: Did you finish your homework?

YOU, SLIGHTLY FRUSTRATED AND WITH A SLIGHT TILT UP IN YOUR VOICE: Grandma, yes. I said I finished it thirty minutes ago.

GRANDMA: Ehh, so you're yelling. Óyá come and beat me.

Sis, how did it escalate so quickly? How did my slight annoyance become "In fact, go get a belt and beat me"? It was hilarious when you weren't the person on the other end of it. I swear, she would sometimes respond to situations as if she were in her own personal *All My Children* episode. (Which was her favorite soap opera, by the way. That was her show! Maybe it's because the theatrics were right up her alley. When Susan Lucci kept getting nominated for a Daytime Emmy but not winning, I think Grandma went to Jesus to intervene. Next thing you know, Susan is standing on that stage holding her award. Amen, saints.)

So Grandma would also pull the "Your own mother wouldn't talk to me like that," which would instantly shame you for the unearned brazenness you showed. Your ego would be knocked down to size.

This line that my grandma drew was known by adults and kids alike. What you not gon' do in the presence of Fúnmi Fáloyin is raise your voice at her in discontent. She'd straight up ask you, "You and who?" It's a question with no real answer, because it's one of those "Lemme make sure you know who you're dealing with" things. And I saw it over and over again, how the most blunt and surly people honored that line of hers. I saw how Nigerian police, who often give no fucks about decorum, would yell at someone in one sentence and speak to my grandmother with such deference and warm tones the next.

It let me know that people are capable of acting like they have sense. They just wield that based on who is in front of them, and what that person has allowed them to get away with. Although it is not our fault when people abuse or disrespect us, how others treat us can be a reflection of what we allow.

At the core of setting boundaries is trying to minimize self-betrayal as we exist in this world. The person who I need to make sure is okay at the end of the day/life is me, because I'm the one I have to answer to, and I'm a critical child of God. Whew! I'm tough, more so on myself than anyone else. And if I gotta tell ME that I somehow bent myself out of shape for someone else, I'ma be mad as hell at myself. I've been mad as hell at me plenty of times before, and I find it really hard to forgive myself. That alone has made me insist on getting better and better at being clear to others about my limits.

I'm usually leery of people who don't have any clear boundaries. Why? Because their lack of boundaries means they are less likely to understand the paint-thick lines that I draw. They might have a hard time with me speaking my limits, seeing it as an act of hostility instead of an act of self-preservation. Plus, they might take my strong boundaries as a lack of transparency and vulnerability. They will have a hard time honoring them. There is an African proverb that says, "Be careful when a naked person offers you a shirt." My structure will make your freewheelingness look like harshness.

One of my biggest boundaries is that I don't like hugging people I don't know. I'm not anti-hugs, because I don't mind waist-bumping folks I know (who also like to be hugged by folks they know)! What I am not a huge fan of is squeezing the body of someone whose name I am not familiar with. This is a tough boundary to have. Why? Because people love to hug! It is a sign of kinship, friendliness, and sometimes kindness. And I, as someone who has a book and is somewhat visible and relatively approachable (when I don't have Resting Side-Eye Face), look pretty huggable. So the fact that I don't really like hugs from people I don't know can make me seem aloof when folks meet me and I decline. And because of that, I find myself letting strangers hug me way more often than I'd like, and then feeling some type of way after.

How it happens: Someone sees me in public (like in the airport) and they're excited and I'm honored! They go, "I'm a hugger!" I wanna respond with "I'm a Capricorn!" since we're shouting out random attributes. I see their smiles, and it makes it that much more difficult to say, "I'd prefer to fist bump." (With COVID-19 and learning how few people wash their hands, I don't even wanna shake hands anymore.) But a lot of times, I'm not even given the choice in the hug. My reflexes are slower than I'd like, and before I can say anything, I'm face-deep in the bosom of a woman who loves my work. I'm both honored and slightly taken aback. I walk away feeling a bit surly.

In that case, when meeting someone who really likes me, I'm afraid to disappoint them or hurt their feelings. The easier choice is to accept the hug. But easier for who? Not me. If it's a day when I'm at a conference speaking, I could be doing that two hundred more times. One paper cut isn't bad, but two hundred might hurt like hell. I'm not comparing hugs from strangers to paper cuts. OR AM I?

Hugs feel very personal to me. This is why I'm not giving them to everyone I meet. This is also why they're such a tough boundary. People take it personally because it probably feels like a personal rejection. I fully understand how someone could feel slighted by being told that their gesture isn't welcome. However, it's one of those "it's not you, it's me" situations. As an experienced introvert, I find my energy sapped by people. Peopling makes me tired, and I usually have to recharge after doing it a lot. Hugs are Super Saiyan levels of peopling when they go into the hundreds. Protect your space and energy in the decent ways you know how.

I've asked people what the best way to decline a hug is. A large number told me to say, "Oh, I have a cold." Or "I'm not feeling well." Soooo the answer to telling people about what I want is to lie? Nah. Why do we need to betray ourselves in that way, by creating a false moment in order to receive the response? Who does it serve? The person who wants the hug? Okay. Meanwhile, now you're having to fake sniffles. All for what? To prevent the discomfort of someone who feels like they should receive a body squeeze from you. I don't even think the means justify the end.

Others told me to make sure I'm holding something in both hands to avoid hugs. Or do a quick *Matrix* backbend to avoid people's grasps. So I gotta be flexible, doing yoga and training with Mr. Miyagi at home to practice and get quicker reflexes to avoid folks' arms around me. Won't it be easier to be able to say, "Hey, I'd prefer not to do that, person whose name I don't know"?

Even the hugging expectation is super gendered. Boys' and men's personal space is often respected. Girls and women are supposed to be the nurturers, and our bodies seem to be community property, so we're expected to wanna hug folks at will. NAWL.

Many of us were not allowed to draw our boundaries growing up, especially with family. We've all seen it or had it done to us: a family member would visit, and we'd be forced to hug them. In those moments, we learned that being related to someone dominates our agency of our own bodies and personal space, and we started thinking that we did not have the right to make choices for our comfort. These small moments have far-reaching impact on how we move through the world. What we learned was that others can impose on us as they wish, and we don't have a say in it. I want you to unlearn that. I want to give you permission to choose what works for you. I want you to say a thoughtful "no" to hugging people you don't want to. You don't have to hug anyone you don't want to. Your body is yours to use as you wish.

We normalize constant betrayal of our needs and ourselves and others around us when we do not take boundaries seriously. Sometimes, the adults around us normalize that too. We act as if everyone has access that we can't revoke, no matter how terribly they treat us or show up. It is not necessarily our fault, but it is our problem to deal with.

While drawing strong lines in person can be hard, even electronically it can be hard to create the boundaries we need. Because again, we prioritize everyone else's harmony over ours.

Social media is the land of crossed boundaries, because there is something about being behind a keyboard that makes people forget all their home training. Folks stay acting out on there!

Since boundaries are my favorite things, right under wing-tip shoes and red velvet cupcakes, I have a lot of them regarding how people should interact with me online. And I very quickly realized that in order for me to not have my entire nerves be tapped on by people and their good intent, it was important for me to make loud PSAs about what my lines were.

There are a few things that really grind my gears and cross my virtual boundaries.

- When people tag me in photos I'm not in, just to get my attention—this is the virtual version of cold-calling me to tell me about your event.

- When people tag me in photos I'm not in, just to get my audience's attention—this taps on the shoulders of those who follow me. It's like putting a billboard on my lawn.

- When people direct message (DM) me to ask for a favor when they've never messaged me before—this is like walking up to a random stranger on the street and asking them to buy the T-shirt you're selling. Can you at least say hi first and introduce yourself? It always feels like some sort of invasion when the ask is money. I've had someone ask me to pay for their tuition before, and it felt like someone reached directly into my pocket rummaging for cash.

All of this is not to say don't talk to me. Rather, it is to say treat me like a person you want to build a relationship with, not someone to take advantage of. Asking for help or a favor is not the problem. The problem is doing it without regard for creating real rapport.

What happens on social media is both a gift and a curse. Because we are all now two degrees separated at most, we feel like everyone is accessible. At its best, this allows us to forge deep connections with people we might never have known otherwise. At its worst, it makes us forget that behind the names and profile pictures are real people. If we kept in mind that we are not entitled to anyone's space, time, or energy, we'd act like we have broughtupsy.

As an early adopter of social platforms, I've known the importance of curating the space I want for years, because our experience in these mediums is wholly dependent on who we let into our eHouses. The people we friend, follow, and like determine the quality of the time we spend scrolling. You might look up one day and find that logging into Instagram or TikTok stresses you out. If your eyes bulge out your face and you want to drop-kick everyone in the face, you should know that it is time to do a digital purge.

Facebook, for example, allows you to have 5,000 friends. Just because that is the maximum doesn't mean that is the number you should have. Just because your house can safely fit one hundred people in it doesn't mean that is the number you should invite for dinner today. We don't control a lot in life, but we can manage who we let into our virtual spaces more than we do.

So you know I got rules for how I accept social media connections.

FACEBOOK

I know Facebook is passé for you, cuz that's where me and the other folks who remember when websites took three minutes to load hang. If you are on there, treat this as the summer picnic of social media. Ask yourself: Have I met you in real life? Do I actually know you by face, and if I see you walking and a road is between us, will I make a point to cross the street to come greet you, or will I duck behind cars so you won't see me?

Why is this important? Well, if I don't want to cheerfully acknowledge you in person and would rather do calisthenics to avoid you, then why do I need to see your posts in my timeline? UN-FRIEND the randoms!

TWITTER

Twitter is the equivalent of an after-school club on social media. Ask yourself: Would I maintain more than a five-minute conversation with you if we met at a program? In this place, where everyone is talking and I'm moving from conversation to conversation, would I keep a conversation with you because I find you fascinating? This is relevant, as it's a space where we're sharing thoughts, opinions, news. I want my timeline to be useful, funny, timely, and interesting. This is also where you might wanna avoid the person who believes the world is flat.

INSTAGRAM

Instagram is the house party of social media. Ask yourself: Would I sit through a slideshow of your last vacation pictures? I'm on Instagram to let my hair down, be a little bit more open about my day-to-day, and share the highlights of my world and thoughts. Sometimes the highlights include lowlights too. It's a platform that allows us to be both professional and personal. The folks I wanna follow there have to be intriguing to me on some level.

TIKTOK

Listen, I only occupy the Auntie section of TikTok, where I avoid the dances so I don't embarrass my nieces. I don't know how y'all decide who to follow there, but my advice would be that you only follow the people who don't make you roll your eyes to the back of your head because they try too hard to do trends. IDK. That's all I got there.

There are people I know in real life who I would not add on Facebook. There are people I don't even know and have never met who I follow on Instagram. There are folks who I wouldn't necessarily break bread with whose tweets are my must-reads. Our social media choices can be personal, even when we say they aren't. I can like you as a person but hide you in my feed if your work tires me out or saps my energy.

Across the board, I don't typically follow or friend complete strangers. In the times when I do hit "follow" on someone I've never met, it's because I feel connected to them in some way. I saw their post and I liked it. Or they left a comment or two that made me laugh. We often say there are no strangers in the world. I agree when people make themselves organically familiar. This doesn't include the trolls who comment under every picture you post saying, "Follow me." You already know I ain't for that. Block block block.

With the strong criteria I have for how I let folks into my eLife, you might be saying, "Wait, but doesn't that mean you'll only be following people who are just like you?" It absolutely can, if the only people I follow are thirty-five-year-old Nigerian Americans with short hair who grew up exactly as I did. But somehow, I still don't think all I have are people who think exactly like me! We can disagree, but what everyone who I let in has in common is that they care about humankind and on a basic level are decent human beings. I find them to be mostly kind, smart, and funny.

The people who are racist, sexist homophobes who are transphobic aren't the ones I allow in. And when they slip through, I fix that quickly by removing our connection. If, in an attempt to not create an echo chamber, we let these folks live in our electronic villages, we're almost vouching for their foolishness.

I also do not let hate or slurs fly in my eSpaces. One of the things I'm most proud of is my audience (shout-out to LuvvNation) and the energy of my platforms. While the rest of the internet can often be a dumpster fire, my comments section is the opposite. It is something that I speak about often, because the people who read my work tout it. The community I've built over the years of writing online knows that if my name is attached to a space, I expect you to show up correct. That means being thoughtful and not a hateful shrew. People say half the fun of my work is my words, and the other half is the comments in response.

In the moments when something I write goes viral, and it's shared on troll pages and I see my space overrun by the type of people who make you lose faith in humans, my audience handles it before I even have a chance. Seeing how protective they are of the safety of the space lets me know I've done something right.

This is also why I am not shy about deleting foolishness that people bring to my space online. My social media is a dictatorship, not a democracy. I block, report as spam, and mute as needed. I am not obligated to receive or consume debris that someone drops at my feet. I take it out the back and throw it in the ether. I'm not the United States government, so speech that I deem daft does not have freedom to live on my platforms.

We spend a lot of our time, online and in real life, having our boundaries crossed. And we stay silent. Why? Because we might think we're making a big deal out of nothing. Or we question whether we're being crotchety. Or we wonder if it will make us less likable since we will be asking someone to do something different.

Well, if it's getting on your nerves, why shouldn't you say so? It is for the betterment of you and whoever is on the other end. When someone crosses my boundaries the first time, I assume it's because they didn't know. So then I tell them. If they do it over and over again after they have been told, I assume they don't care. At that point, my action to remove them from my life is blameless. I done told you, but you ain't listen. When people don't respect your boundaries after you've told them, remove them from your space without guilt. They don't get access to you anymore.

People will not like it when you start establishing and enforcing your drawn lines. They'll feel like you built a gate to keep THEM out, instead of seeing it as a gate to keep anything that doesn't serve you out. They might take it personally, and there's gonna be very little you can do about that.

I remember receiving a note from someone who was mad that she couldn't comment on my personal Facebook page. She felt like I was "keeping people at bay." I replied back with "I have a public fan page, a Twitter account, an Instagram account. And I cannot keep some semblance of privacy on my personal page? That is a lot of access. Can't help that you feel that way. It is what it is."

These things aren't only online occurrences. I was at a friend's personal event, stuffing my face with food, when someone came up to me to ask for a hug and a selfie. And I said I'd do it once I finished eating. She got offended and let a mutual friend know that I wasn't nice. Maybe I should have dapped her up and kept it moving, but I thought I was being "nice" by saying I'd do it after I finished chewing food. But nah, she still got upset. That lesson is: Don't be afraid of not being nice, because people will take from an interaction whatever they want. It is out of your control, good intentions and all.

When you draw boundaries, people might say you've changed and you think you're somehow better than them. They might say you are not nice. Let them. In fact, they will be saying it from afar because it won't be to your face since your drawn lines are so good, they won't be able to reach you. Preserve your sanity, because even if you try to bend yourself backward for folks, they'll still say you didn't do enough. You don't OWE anyone your time, energy, or platform. Do not feel guilty about being protective of any of those things.

Before I got married, my VERY strong boundary was not to speak about my relationship or whether I was even in one. As a result, folks who were nosy created stories about my love life, my sexual orientation, and whatever else they wanted to fill in the gap on. All I asked of folks was that whoever they thought I was dating (he/she/they) be a bad bitch, and I would be satisfied. PLEASE start a rumor that I had an affair with Rihanna. That'd be lit!

When I got engaged, I posted a picture of me and my boo (now husband) on social. The post went up five days after it happened, because I wanted to take my time and not rush breaking boundaries I wasn't even fully comfortable with. Before I posted, I asked myself, "Argh! Now do people have to know?" But I said yes, because my ring was gonna tell on me, so lemme tell on myself. When the post went up, it got SO MUCH ATTENTION. I got 54,000 likes and 8,800 comments. I have done a lot in my life and accomplished a lot. The engagement post is the one that garnered the most likes and comments EVER for me. It was overwhelming. I remember people being like, "OMG I didn't even know she was dating someone." It's possible to be visible and still keep some of our spaces to ourselves.

While I'm here, lemme advise you to create some boundaries around what you will post on these internets. You do not have to be an incredibly sanitized or boring version of yourself online. You can still show the most colorful, funny side of who you are without jeopardizing scholarships, college admissions, or other opportunities. But if you wouldn't want something you posted to end up on a jumbotron in Times Square, DO NOT POST IT or send it as a text message. Do not post something on the internet that you wouldn't want to see on a billboard. Do not send text messages or pictures that couldn't be plastered on a school chalkboard. Even adults need to hear this. Draw those lines as you engage on social platforms.

Remember: your life is not a carnival, and not everyone should get a ticket to it. I see my own life as a highly exclusive club (where there are beds and the rice flows and no one has to wear heels or uncomfortable clothes), and the ones who come in are on the guest list. They are the people I know are a good time and won't start a fight. The cool thing is, if someone rowdy comes in, I can kick 'em out at any time. Remember: Not everyone gets a ticket to your life. This is YOUR club, so you have the right to have whoever you want in there. You can draw your lines by letting people go.

Let go of the friends that don't really have your back and the crush/boyfriend/girlfriend who makes you feel bad about yourself. You are not obligated to keep toxic people around you, even if you do have to see them at school. When people purposefully do not respect your boundaries, let them go from having immediate access to your time, energy, and dopeness.

Draw lines, even if the person is family. Honestly, it's especially important to know you can have boundaries with the people you love. These are the folks we feel most obligated to bend till we break for. These are the ones who can manipulate us to erase the boundaries that are most important to our well-being. These are the ones who early on teach us that our feelings aren't worth protecting because we are erroneously obligated through blood connection.

Do not get to the point where you give everyone everything you have, in terms of energy and time and brain power and money and even your presence. Because what will happen is you will be left with nothing and they will still have everything that you gave them.

Know that you have the right to have your preferences, your borders, your boundaries. Tell people outright that you prefer another type of behavior. Wear a T-shirt. Make PSAs. Use a hashtag. Feel no guilt about it. Prevent riffraffery and the enemies of progress from constantly piercing your territory. Build a wall to keep tomfoolery out.

Draw your lines without guilt.

DO

We can't be all talk with no action. In this DO section,
let's start doing the things that might seem scary.

"GROW ANYWAY. DO WHAT'S HARD ANYWAY. CHANGE ANYWAY."

—Luvvie Ajayi Jones

10

FIND YOUR HELPERS

We fear betrayal.

 Although we spend our lives looking for the approval of others, we are also afraid of building community. But the thing is, we NEED people.

Humans are not meant to do life alone. Even the most introverted and crotchety of us is not meant to be a recluse, living life away from everyone with no one to turn to. When people are imprisoned, there is a reason why the biggest punishment is solitary confinement. To lock a person away from all human contact is to torture them.

We need people to cheer for us, encourage us, challenge us, scold us, love us, be there for us. We need people to be our HELPERS.

But we are afraid to need people. We are afraid of being

deceived or double-crossed. The fear of that hurt often keeps us from building deep relationships in the way we need to. We are afraid of being rejected, and that's a form of betrayal, ain't it? We are afraid of giving people the power to punch us in the proverbial chest because we've let them get close. Some of us have parents who have beat it into our heads to "trust no one." We carry their traumas as ours. We wear their fears as ours before we can even understand the world in its most basic ways.

But again, empires of one aren't built, and neither is a fulfilling life that only includes you. Let people help you. Mr. Rogers said, "When I was a boy and I would see scary things in the news, my mother would say to me, 'Look for the helpers. You will always find people who are helping.'"

To find your helpers is to squad up. To squad up is to form community. It is to create bonds and friendships and acquaintanceships with others, allowing them access to us. And those people can then be accomplices in our lives, in our dreams being realized, and in our journey to becoming the dopest versions of ourselves.

The thing we are afraid of about having helpers is that we are afraid of being betrayed and let down. Like a lot of our other fears, this betrayal one is valid and earned. Humans can be dishonest, selfish, self-centered, and all that other jazz. People are fickle, untrustworthy, sheisty AF. They give us many reasons to wanna lock ourselves in dark rooms and say nothing to anyone ever again. Sometimes, the drama that people bring into our lives tempts us into thinking, *Forget everyone. I'ma just be by myself.* I get it. But humans, at our best, are soft places to land.

There is one person I trust above all else in this world: me, myself, and I. I've spent a lifetime depending on myself, getting things done no matter what, and making the impossible seem easy. That trust I have in myself has led to so many wins that my faith in myself is massive. It's why I'm harder on me than anyone else can ever be. It's why I think I could climb mountains if I really focused. It's why I wrote this book. I trust me so hard. That's all ego.

But it can be a detriment. Self-reliance, just like anything else, can be a problem when there's too much of it. What we call independence and self-sufficiency is often us operating from a place of fearing losing control. What happens when we depend on other people and they let us down? What happens if we put something in someone else's hands and they drop the ball? What happens when we lose something because we trusted it to someone else? We run that scenario over and over again and find ourselves doing everything ourselves. It is exhausting!

But really. What are the consequences of us living life, carrying responsibilities purely on our backs? Plainly, we tire ourselves out, when we could be allowing our HELPERS to pick up slack for us before we drown in overwhelm.

We have to fire ourselves from the idea that we can do it all alone, without anyone's help, no matter how strong we think we are. We need FAMILY (chosen or otherwise), FRIENDS, MENTORS, CLASSMATES to get through this life. And we need to not be shy about seeking them out. They are LIFE HELPERS.

My grandmother Mama Fáloyin was a FIERCE woman, in all ways. She really did know how to take up room without apology. Once, in Nigeria, she was in the car as my uncle drove and one of my aunts was in the front seat. They got cut off by another driver, and instead of him being apologetic, he started cussing at them. My uncle pulls over and gets out. You'd think my grandmother would be the peacekeeper. NOPE. This woman jumped out the car herself, grabbed the driver by his shirt, and threatened to fight him and the person who was in the car with him. At the end of it all, the driver and his passenger ended up prostrating at her feet to apologize for disrespecting her.

How did she become this chick? Well, having to fend for herself since the age of eighteen probably made her grow some seriously tough skin. And somewhere along the way, she curated a squad of other tough-ass, take-no-shit Nigerian women. These women LIVED. They didn't discourage her from taking up space. In fact, her crew of fellow professional troublemakers hyped her up and affirmed her in the times when she had to put on pants and let someone have it! At her sixtieth birthday, they were right next to her, in their own specific fabric, looking like the proud, territorial friends we all want. I think they all coordinated their "sunglasses even though it's nighttime" look.

Bold women rock with other bold women because we create space for each other and affirm identities society is usually quick to denounce. We normalize each other's bravado, which allows us to step into the world with confidence. It's almost to the point where if you don't stand up with your head tall, you'll feel slightly out of place. The badassery of my friends usually reminds me who the hell I am and why I need to keep my chin square, and that is a gift I've gratefully received and will continue to.

The people we are surrounded by really do affirm our lives and our decisions. They can peer-pressure us into being and doing better, because seeing them up close can inspire us to know what's possible. You also need a strong village to hold you up in the times when you can't stand up straight. When people who you will never meet call you all types of scallywags, your squad will remind you of who you are. When you doubt everything you know about you, they bring you back to what you stand for. The real ones don't go running after you fall on your ass. Who is there taking your hand and pulling you back on your feet? Remember them.

My accomplishments might be half because of my drive and the other half because I don't come from half-stepping people. The people who I love do amazing things, so that's also my job. If they were slackers, maybe I'd feel less pressure to always GO. Without competition or envy, we can compare ourselves to them with the lens of "Well, if it's possible for her, it's possible for me."

As I discussed in chapter 1, it is integral that we know whose we are. Who do we come from? Who do we claim? Who do we belong to? This WHO isn't just about the last names we carry or the legacy of our lineage. I firmly affirm the fact that I belong to a crew of dope-ass friends too.

Entrepreneur Jim Rohn made popular the idea of "You are the sum of the five closest people to you." This rings true to me. Even if that number isn't five, I am the sum of the villages of people who have surrounded me throughout my life. How far I've been able to go has been directly tied to those people. How smooth or rocky my journey is has been because of those people. How big I dream has been because of their confidence.

Even beyond the gassing up of each other, I find so much value in how my friends are my greatest challengers. We take "My Sister's Keeper" or "My Brother's Keeper" literally. My journey is a testament to me being afraid but helpers in the form of friends and mentors and my partner not letting me cower in the face of fear.

There are so many rewards to building a proper village that the accompanying fear isn't worth it. Throughout my life, I've felt betrayed and abandoned and rejected by people who I let into my life. We've all felt it. It's knocked me on my ass a few times. But I also think about what others have done for me or said to me that has lifted me up or pushed me forward. Those moments beat any of the betrayals. Those times attest to the need to never harden myself completely.

One of my friends is the reason I said YES to doing the TED Talk I did that went viral with over seven million views. She was my HELPER at a time when I was doubting myself and my abilities, loaning me courage I didn't have for myself in that moment. Her name is Eunique, and she changed my life, simply with one sentence.

Back in July 2017, I was invited to speak at TEDWomen by curator Pat Mitchell (legendary journalist and correspondent). I had wanted to do an official TED Talk for a while, but I was already booked for a different conference in a different city that day, so I hit a *wall slide* and declined. Two weeks before TEDWomen (which was happening November 1), I got the schedule for the other conference, and it turned out that the only thing happening the first day was an optional VIP party. I was like, "Maybe I can drop by TEDWomen in New Orleans for a day to cheer on my friends and then head to New York." So I messaged the TED team and let them know I'd like to have a day pass to the conference. Upon which they were like, "Why don't you come speak?" And I was like, "WAIT, WHAT?!?" Pat wanted me to take the stage while I was there.

And this is where I panicked and did the thing that is a surefire way to hustle backward: I let fear dictate my decision-making.

Here's the thing: TED is really picky about speakers and preparation. People get coaches, talks are vetted, and when you take that stage, you have been prepped extensively for it. Those talks don't soar for no reason. There is a lot of work put behind them! So, here I am, two weeks before a TED event, being asked to take the stage. I was in my head like, WHAT ABOUT MY COACHES? I DON'T EVEN HAVE A TALK YET. OMG, TWO WEEKS IS NOTHING.

I didn't wanna take that stage and bomb. NOPE. So I decided that I was gonna decline (again) and tell Pat I'd be in the audience cheering. I wrote out a three-paragraph email expressing my regret about how I needed to pass on it because I was swamped and didn't want to bring less than 100 percent to their stage. I was afraid I would fail with flying colors. Right before I hit "send" on the email, I decided to call my girl Eunique Jones Gibson. She's a valued member of my life village, and I just needed to hear her tell me that I was making the right decision by saying NO.

ME: They asked me to do a TED Talk and it's in like a week and a half and I think I'll decline because I'm not ready. Everyone else has had months to practice, and coaches, and here I am sliding in the eleventh hour.

EUNIQUE: Well, you ain't everybody.

ME: Well, damb.

EUNIQUE: You've been on a stage twice a week for the last six weeks. You've been speaking professionally for almost a decade. Everything you've done up until now has been your coach. Everything has prepared you for this. You're ready.

ME: Whoa.

EUNIQUE: And if they didn't think you could do it, they wouldn't have asked you. You are doing it.

ME: Gahtdamb. Drag me, then! My edges. Here, take them.

EUNIQUE: Aight, get off my phone and go prepare for your TED Talk. Kill it. *hangs up*

Bruh, she got me SO TOGETHER. I went in my email and deleted the draft I was gonna send Pat. The next day, I wrote my talk. While I was in an Uber on the way to the airport for another trip. I hit "send" on it as the car pulled up to O'Hare airport. I thought they'd hate the talk and tell me to sit it out. NOPE. They loved it.

Then they told me I needed to be in New Orleans two days before the conference so I could practice, which was required of speakers. I couldn't be in NOLA until the morning of November 1 because I was getting an award in Chicago the day before (brag on yourself, folks!). I was like, "Well, here's the part where they kick me out, which is fine." But instead they were like, "Ah. Well, let's do video rehearsal then."

Oh, and the conference was starting at 6:00 p.m. on November 1. To make my other conference, I had to take the last flight out, which was at 8:00 p.m. I let them know, thinking, "Okay, this is the last straw." Pat replied by telling me it was no problem, and they would make sure I was the opening speaker at TEDWomen so I could make that flight.

Every time I thought they'd be like, "This ain't gon' work. Thanks but no thanks," they found a work-around to another one of my (valid) excuses. I MEAN. Talk about votes of confidence.

The night before the talk, I was at home rehearsing it to an audience of one: my husband, Carnell. He was like, "This is pretty good, but I think it's missing something." So I sat down at my computer and started changing things. Before I knew it, I changed half of the talk. The new version of this talk was one that infused more of my story. It was better. Much better.

The next morning, I hopped on the flight to New Orleans, exhausted because I got so little sleep from reworking my talk and from being the last-minute packer that I am. I was on that flight looking downtrodden, with tote bags under my eyes. But instead of sleeping, I put my head against the window and repeated my talk to myself over and over again, because I had decided to do it from memory, and I still didn't have it memorized.

When I arrived, I kept reading my script and going through it my head, because I wasn't using any prompts besides the slides that would run behind me. There was no confidence monitor or tele-prompter that would help me. I was spooked because this wasn't a talk I had given before.

I usually don't get too nervous when I'm about to give talks, but for this? I WAS NERVOUS AF. And I was going to be the first speaker!

The time for my talk arrived. And I stepped on that TED stage and gave the talk of my life! In ten minutes, I dropped over 1,700 words, challenging people to be truth-tellers committed to doing and saying what was difficult because that is necessary for us to move forward. In it, I used myself as the example, how my life changed when I decided to stop being led by fear. I used the idea of being a domino, because the first one to fall inspires others to do the same.

Ten minutes and fifty-four seconds straight through. No stops. The TED Talk I gave is the one you can watch now. There was no editing magic. My voice did not shake. It poured out of me like I had been doing that very talk for years.

I said my last sentences: "It is our job, it is our obligation, it is our duty to speak truth to power. To be the domino, not just when it's difficult—especially when it's difficult. Thank you."

I immediately ran off the stage because I had not forgotten that I had a plane to catch (it was 6:25 p.m. at that time). But before I could leave, the stage manager turned me around and said, "I need you to go back out there and see the standing ovation you're getting right now." And I walked back and saw people on their feet cheering for me.

I was overwhelmed in the best way. I coulda cried, but I didn't have time! I took a bow and ran right back off the stage. I jumped in the car and made it to the airport by 7:10 p.m. I ran through the airport and made that 8:00 p.m. flight with thirty minutes to spare. On the flight, I was exhausted but geeked. I was geeked, y'all. I knew I killed it. I had done something to be proud of.

A week later, I got an email saying they would like to feature my talk on TED.com's homepage on December 1. I coulda fallen off my chair, because TED doesn't guarantee when talks go up. Some don't see the light of day for six months after they happen, and mine was picked to go up in less than a month.

And surely, when that day came, "Getting Comfortable with Being Uncomfortable" was front and center on the TED homepage. Within a month, the talk had received one million views. And now, it has been watched over seven million times and is still growing. Most importantly, the messages I've been getting from all over the world, from people who let me know how my talk spurred them to take an action they might not have otherwise, have stuck with me.

This talk that changed my life? I almost didn't do it. I wouldn't have if it weren't for my helpers in the form of Pat Mitchell (who believed so deeply in me and didn't let my excuses get in her belief), Eunique (who recognized my power in a moment of self-doubt and did not let me say NO), and Carnell (who challenged me to show up as my best self through the talk).

My helpers helped me do the thing that changed my life (and changed the lives of countless others who watched it).

Imagine if any of them had not done their part to push me forward. Imagine how my life would be different if they'd let me let fear win. Imagine what I would have missed out on in not taking that stage and being bold and vulnerable.

When I say "find your helpers," I don't mean "ask everyone you meet for something." One of the reasons people struggle with friendships and romantic relationships is that they expect everyone in their lives to fulfill all their needs. We expect friends to mentor us, play hard with us, challenge us, be our shoulders to cry on. Yes, our friends are supposed to do that, but no one or two people can do or be all of that for you. You have to spread that responsibility around.

We are less likely to experience the deep betrayals and the rejections if we understand that people serve certain purposes and not everyone can be in the same role with the same expectations.

I think there are four types of helpers that we all need.

1. THE DAY ONES

The Day Ones are the friends you've had since you were younger. They can pull out embarrassing pics of you at any time, since they have ample. They remember when you cut your own bangs in kindergarten and can humble you in a hot second. Remember when you had chicken pox in the second grade? They do! They have the proof. They also might call you by a nickname that no one else knows now. Why is it important to have these people? Because they're a mirror of who you were. They give you perspective, and as you're meeting new people or getting grown, they are a reminder of how far you've come and of the person you used to be when you were still dreaming of who you are today. They are a grounding force.

2. THE SCHOOL CREW

These are the people you've bonded with at school. Y'all grab lunch together and have a bunch of classes together. They might cover for you when you miss an important class or give you a heads-up about a test that's coming up. Your shared experience makes these friends important, because they can look out for you at the place you spend most of your days. And all that time spent together means you can vent to them about things that you might not want to bore anyone else with. They are the reason your school experience is what it is.

3. THE MENTORS

Mentors are the life version of "not your little friends." They are essential because even though they aren't your peers, they can be life rafts. Your parents are probably your first mentors, but look beyond them. A mentor might take the form of a favorite teacher who looks out for you and your well-being, even after you no longer take their class. They might champion your work and make sure you have what you need to succeed academically. Because mentors care about your life, you can confide in them. They're guides who aren't your guardians.

Mentors are incredible, because they can unlock doors in our lives. They can make our dreams more tangible, because they are invested in our success. You need an internship? Well, they might be able to make a phone call to someone who then makes a phone call to get you the interview you need. You need a scholarship?

They found out about one that won't even be posted, and they told you in advance so you can get your paperwork done. They actively ask "How can I help?" without necessarily expecting anything.

The domino effect mentors have is amazing. It was a mentor of mine (Barbara Allen) who nominated me for the Chicago inaugural chapter of New Leaders Council, which I got accepted for. It was there that I wrote a vision statement, three months before I got fired/laid off from my job, that allowed me to see my dreams on paper.

And many of those dreams have been realized. Barbara nominated me simply because she thought it would be good for me to have that cohort experience. My mentors have brought up my name in rooms and gotten me opportunities I wouldn't be able to get myself. They have opened locked doors.

4. THE TRUE BLUES

We've all heard that if you end up with two or three people in this category, consider yourself blessed, which is a word. The besties are an important subgroup, and everyone ain't that.

The True Blues are the people who know where all the bodies are buried, because they were probably right there with the shovel next to us. We can be our truest selves with them, without pretense or angst. They've seen us at our worst but hold space for us to make it back to our best selves. They will fight for us, even without our permission. They will come to our house and open our fridge like they live there. Your mom probably asks you how they're doing, and sometimes she doesn't because they've called her already. The inside jokes are plenty, and they've seen you in the morning when you still had eye crusties.

Our True Blues aren't automatically the people we've known the longest. They are people who showed up somehow, at some point, and barreled their way into our hearts. We don't know how to NOT trust them, because they've shown us over and over again that they are here to stay. Sometimes they'll disappoint us and upset us, because we are all flawed. But you already know life isn't about perfection.

Each of these groups is essential to having a well-rounded village and is fundamental to our well-being. And these groups are dynamic. Just because someone started in one box doesn't mean that is where they will remain. I have a few friends I met professionally who became True Blues over time.

Everyone ain't gonna come on this life journey with us, and the squads we have today will not necessarily be the friends we have tomorrow. As we get older, our relationships change. We leave some people behind.

When we fear finding helpers, we fear betrayal, and it's real. Do not trust EVERYONE. Sure. But "trust no one" is the quickest way to build titanium walls that no one can break through. Either we learn to let the bridge down for those who are allies or we keep the wall up, protecting ourselves from both the ones who want to see us fall and the ones who will fight for us to keep us standing. Sure, walls keep the villains out, but they also keep the heroes out. In the process of being vigilant against the sheisters, we keep ourselves from connecting with the best people. So I take the worthwhile risk.

O ur lives ain't meant to be lived alone. Even our dreams aren't meant to be realized with no one's help.

I think of my grandmother, Mama Fáloyin. She was as self-reliant as they came. Fire herself? NEVER. Who? A whole her. No. She even used to tell my grandfather that she didn't need him, to remind him that she could handle whatever with or without his help. Grandpa was a man of few words, so he'd just blank-stare her till she tired herself out from ranting.

My grandmother was widowed in 1991, and as she got older, she began to rely more and more on her kids and grandkids. She got diagnosed with diabetes when she turned sixty-four and had to start taking medication for the first time. The years went by, and age made her shrink a bit physically and she couldn't move around freely like she used to. A few years later, she had a stroke, and one of my aunts had to go to Nigeria to bring her to the United States to get treatment. The woman who used to hop on a plane to head anywhere whenever she wanted was now unable to even speak, let alone travel unaccompanied.

I remember visiting her in the hospital one day and being taken aback by how helpless and fragile she seemed. The fierce dynamo I was so accustomed to couldn't even feed herself. The tears came before I could stop them.

The doctor told us that she might never talk again, and I think my grandma took it as a dare. A couple of months later, her speech was back to 100 percent. The stroke she wasn't supposed to recover from seemed like an extended hiccup. But after that, my grandmother started letting people do things for her in a way she hadn't previously. It must have been a jarring thing for her to experience.

After she recovered here for a year, she wanted to be back at her own house doing her thing, so she returned to Nigeria. She had house help staying there with her, had other people running errands for her, and seemed less intense about controlling day-to-day things. My mom would call her and ask her what she was eating and if she was taking her meds. Before, Grandma might have been annoyed about being fussed over in that way, but by then, she realized it was a show of love.

It was another twelve years before we lost her. But whenever Mama Fáloyin was in the US, she'd come and stay with us, even though we lived in a small apartment. My mom would regulate her food, meal planning for her to make sure she wasn't snacking as she liked—her sugar intake had to be leveled. Grandma couldn't go on her random shopping trips for hours like she used to (this was before everyone had cell phones, so we didn't want anything to happen and she couldn't reach us). The lady basically had a curfew, and she didn't even trip. When she got cataracts in both her eyes and couldn't get surgery on them until they matured, she needed my mom to help her arrange her pill box.

I remember one day, she came to me and said, "Tell your mom I said thank you. She takes really good care of me. God will continue to bless her." It was with so much appreciation. I'm a useless somebody, though. I'm not sure I relayed the message. But my mother knew her mother's gratitude, because she heard it herself. This lifelong soldier had dropped the reins and allowed herself to be fully in the hands of someone else. It was a show of strength, in her moment of weakness, to surrender herself to someone she knew would not let her fall.

If love is a verb, is there a greater show of love than to abdicate your very being to the person you raised well enough to hold you up? What is pride when we can have love shown to us instead?

I hope that one day, we are surrounded by people who we trust enough to HELP US, especially in our darkest moments. I pray that I'll have lived a life that's so good I'll be blessed with people who are a reflection of it. And those people, if needed, can be entrusted with my very life. I aspire to live in a way where I attract that favor.

Trust life. Yes, it's a raving douchecanoe at times. But trust the universe/God. Sometimes I think half my reason for believing in a deity is so I don't lose hope and think life is a random mixture of arbitrary instances and none of it has any structure. That might drive me mad. I choose to believe in a higher being as an anchor and a grounding. I don't think I have a choice but to have deep belief that it will work out. It lets me get out of bed even when I'm feeling low.

If control is a mirage, trust that God will order your steps. Have faith that Allah will place the right people in your path: the helpers. One of my favorite prayers is "Let my helpers find me." It is an ask, a prayer, and an affirmation. It is short but full of intention. We think humility is diminishing our gifts. I think it is opening our hearts to the help we deserve and need in the world.

To say "Let my helpers find me" is to ask the universe/God to make you a magnet for blessings through other people. It is a prayer that is always answered, because I am perpetually surrounded by people who insist on being trail lighters for me, and for that I'm always grateful.

The companion prayer is "Let me be able to receive their help."

My success is from my hard work and gifts. But it is also from the times I've been able to receive God's grace in the form of other people's service to me. My journey is a testament to people who have spoken my name up in rooms I'm not in, mentored me through difficult moments, and said YES to me as others have said no. I am the culmination of moments where people have loaned me their courage. I am walking proof of "community is a verb."

May you always be surrounded by helpers. Not only may you find them, but may they seek you out. May you find ease in your life from the hands of others.

11

GROW WILDLY

We fear change.

 Change is scary because we are afraid of the unknown. We like what is familiar because that is what is comfortable and what we know intimately.

I come to you, as Change-Averse Club president, because I love control and I love knowing things. The mystery that comes with future things is my kryptonite. You'd think a lifetime of not being psychic would have gotten me used to it by now. But I've been forced to deal with it because I have the nerve to want better things, and I realize how old habits, old ways, and old thoughts won't get me those things.

Let's face it: I am a mess. I mean that in the most self-aware, not-put-downy way possible. Like how Forky from *Toy Story 4* declared, "I am trash!" because he knew it was fact, since he was made of literal garbage. As humans, by default, we are walking compost heaps who are constantly trying God's patience and daring Him/Her/Them to activate another flood. As a species, we're lazy, selfish, self-serving, money-obsessed, climate-killing atomic fragments. The fact that Jesus hasn't come to get us yet, dragging us by our soiled hoodies, is a testimony of praise.

And I am a fool who has put her foot in her mouth more than a couple of times, with a stubborn streak and a perfectionism problem that sometimes requires me to be told to go occupy a seat because I'm doing too much. I'm a piece of work in progress. Can't nobody tell me my flaws because I'll read that tome of a list to you in a hot second.

Humans are sentient sewage sometimes, and what we can do is attempt to not be as scummy as we used to be. This is why one of my life's goals is to not be the same type of trash I was last decade, last year, or last week. I'm probably the same fool I was yesterday, and that's okay. I'll give myself that grace. But tomorrow? I should be better.

What happens when you commit to not being as terrible as you used to be? It means you are going to change. It means you are constantly going to be different from who you used to be, even if only in small ways. It means the only thing that will stay the same is your perpetual evolution. It's that quote from an old dead Greek dude, Heraclitus of Ephesus, epitomized: "Change is the only constant in life." Nobody has proven this wrong yet.

What I know is that who we are right this moment is not who we're going to end up being. Not only should we want to change, it is our duty to change. It is our duty to constantly look to be better than we are. And you know what that is? Growth. Growth is an obligation, and we gotta give ourselves permission to grow wildly, like my cuticles after a month of neglect.

Permission is one thing; execution is another.

Once you know you gotta get doper and better, now comes the part where the ground you stand on will be shaken up. When folks talk about "growing pains," they mean it literally. Change is often not fun. Growth is not always sunshine and rainbows, because it means our comfort zones are going to be pulled away from us. It means what's convenient is not going to be what prevails. It is hard, and that's why it is scary.

This is also why change often happens by force, not by choice. We don't wake up one day and say, "I feel really comfortable, and things are great. I should make a change." That's not typically how it happens. Usually there's a catalyst that coerces us into shifting.

Sometimes it's something external, like our parents getting divorced or changing schools or even going through friendship breakups.

Other times, the force is internal—not a major external moment but our conscience, our spirit. We're feeling bored or we're feeling like we're not in the right place. Or we're feeling unexcited to wake up in the morning because we don't have much we look forward to in our days. Or we're feeling like we are gasping our way through life. Whatever the impetus, internal or external, change can throw us off our feet.

In my life, the moments I've been called to change have been very clear, like moving to the United States when I was nine and having to become the new girl for the first time ever in my life.

Or like the time I got to college, took Chemistry 101, and got the first D of my academic career (see chapter 3). That was when I dropped my premed major and my lifelong dream of being a doctor, and through a series of domino moments became a writer, which led me to this book.

There's the moment when I received major backlash online and learned that I needed to be better as a thinker, as a human, as an intellectual, as somebody with a platform (see chapter 6).

There's me getting married and realizing that I have to be less selfish and less me-me-me, and that I also have to work through my own trauma to make sure I'm not passing it on and projecting it onto my partner.

Each one of these tough moments was deeply uncomfortable, agonizing, with tears (snot bubbles included), and shrouded by struggle. They had me doubting everything I knew to be true. I could feel my emotional bones stretching, and the growing pains felt physical at times.

But each one of these incidents also led me to becoming the person that I am now. Even if I didn't understand it in the moment, change always leads me to something greater. My life is a testimony to the instances when I've been forced to change, and the lessons that I've learned have always been greater than anything I could have imagined. And those lessons were stairs to the person I am now, and who I am now is another step to the person I'm going to be.

There's an Igbo proverb that goes, "A palm nut that wants to become palm oil must pass through fire." "Diamonds are formed under pressure" is another good reminder. YES. To become who you must be, you might have to go through some things!

Growing wildly is sometimes not a choice but a need, because life will give you no other slot. In these moments, we have to know change is as much a part of life as breathing is.

I think about my grandmother. Mama Fáloyin might have once been a chill, patient, soft-spoken person, but I wouldn't know. There's no point in even speculating, because her life was filled with so many abrupt occasions that insisted she change from moment to moment. All of that contributed to the woman who I knew to be tough, fierce, take-no-mess, and loving with all her heart.

Fúnmiláyọ̀ Fáloyin was born in Lagos as Fúnmiláyọ̀ Láṣọ́rè, to David and Celina Láṣọ́rè. David was an educated man, a teacher by trade, while Celina kept the home running. They had five children, and Fúnmi was kid number three. Fọlọ́unshọ́.* followed her. Their last-born died at a young age.

When my grandma was about sixteen or seventeen years old, her life changed completely. Her paternal grandmother was next in line to rule Ọrún Èkìtì,† a town in Èkìtì state, Nigeria. Their lineage had come up in the succession of the throne, but because her grandmother was a woman, she couldn't become king. She thought about her son David and chose him to take her place, since he had the knowledge and the preferred gender of royalty in a patriarchy (yup). Often you are left with very little choice when strong traditions like this call, so my grandmother's parents uprooted their family from the hustle and bustle of Lagos to the rurality of the rituals of Ọrún Èkìtì.

I cannot even imagine what such a disruption to your life would feel like. Overnight, Fúnmiláyọ̀ became a princess, along with her younger sister, Fọlọ́unshọ́. At that point, she was the oldest child still at home, because her two older brothers were out in the world.

Within a year of ascending to the throne, my grandmother's

*Pronounced faw-LAW-oon-SHAW
†Pronounced ay-kee-tee

father, David, died suddenly. Because life can be a summabish sometimes, her mother, Celina, passed away not long after that.

In less than eighteen months, my grandmother's life turned upside down. She went from being a city girl in a household with both of her parents to moving to a town and becoming royalty to becoming an orphan. She had to grow up very quickly from that point because LIFE DOESN'T OFTEN WARN US THAT IT'S ABOUT TO DROP-KICK US IN THE FACE.

As the oldest heir who was traceable, my grandmother was made a regent of Ọrún Èkìtì. A regent is someone who is appointed to rule in the interim as they find a king. She stayed regent for a few months, until they finally found a new king. Can you imagine how an eighteen-year-old who had lost the people most important to her might feel, and then to be told to handle the business of a city? Bruh!

After that, she was moved to Iléṣà, under the charge of her uncle, her dad's younger brother, who happened to be a cartoon villain. His legend preceded him as a man who wasn't only tough but was also cruel. This uncle sold all of her father's property and heirlooms, because nothing enables greed as much as death. Instead of these things coming to my grandma and the remaining siblings, it all went to him. Plus, he set fire to David's house. It's why we don't have any pictures of the Láṣórès. So much burned down with that house.

So Fúnmiláyọ̀, at eighteen, took on parenting her younger

sibling, thirteen-year-old Fọlọunshọ́, while under the control of a man who stole everything that she was entitled to.

Going from having a family of four to only two of them remaining in so little time had to feel like heartbreak whiplash. How could she have even grieved? Did she smile at all in those days? Did she ever think hope was a useless emotion? Did she ever want to give up on everything and wither away? Did she feel equipped to carry on when so much of what and who she knew as her grounding was gone?

She didn't seem to be the giving-up type, even though she kept getting thrown curveballs. Her uncle decided to throw her another one: an arranged marriage. Fúnmiláyọ̀ was informed that she was being betrothed to some older man, so at eighteen, she would be forced to start a family with some stranger.

Since she wasn't given any other option, she created one herself: to run away.

My grandmother took her only remaining sibling and fled Iléṣà to Ìbàdàn, two hours away, to start life over rather than be tied to a man she never knew by a man she probably wished she didn't know. She chose the road that felt freer: starting with nothing. This was 1950, a time when women were still supposed to be YESSIR-ing men who claimed authority over their lives. This teenager, who had been to hell on earth and could have stayed there, decided to trade that hell for another in a city where she didn't really have roots.

In Ìbàdàn, she met my grandfather, Emmanuel Ọládiípọ̀ Fáloyin. It is there that she started the legacy I hail from. It is there that she birthed my mom, Oluyemisi (her third child). It is there that I was born. It is in the family house that she and my grandfather built where I learned that family was my safe harbor. It is there where I became the first version of myself.

Mama Fáloyin's life was full of moments when the old her wouldn't serve her or keep her safe. Her life was full of times when she had to choose to change where she physically was. Her early life was tumultuous enough that she might never even have survived long enough to give birth to the woman who would give me life and allow me to be here.

She HAD to change. Fúnmiláyọ̀ at fifteen, living in Lagos, was not the same person at seventeen in Ọrún Èkìtì. That person at eighteen in Iléṣà was not the same person who then showed up in Ìbàdàn. She wouldn't have survived in Ìbàdàn, so she had to be done away with. But all of those people had to exist to become the sixty-year-old who threw a seven-day party to celebrate six decades of not breaking, even when life tried to snap her in half. Her joy was in knowing what she had to weather to get to where she was. Like Miss Sofia from *The Color Purple*, all her life she had to fight. But she was always victorious.

I think about another set of wise words from Miss Angelou: "You may not control all the events that happen to you, but you can decide not to be reduced by them." Change sometimes shocks us into learning maturity, resilience, and discernment. These are all things we need, but sometimes the reason we're afraid of change is because we're scared of what other people will say. Imagine if my grandma had stayed in Iléṣà because of what people would say about her if she didn't become Random Old Man's wife? Chile, we must DO it anyway. My grandmother was not reduced by those struggles, even as they changed her.

As we are going through life, and people who know us see us grow, we might hear them say, "You've changed." Sometimes, it will hurt our feelings to hear, because that's the intention behind the statement. They're saying that we are no longer the old us and that they don't recognize who we are. But what they're really saying is THEY haven't changed. They might be thinking we aren't on the same level as them anymore and are projecting that onto us. And yeah, it's really easy to be offended by it. We might be tempted to make somebody else feel better and say, "No, I haven't changed. I'm still the same person." We would be wrong. We did change. We tried something new. We got new results. We changed our worlds. Maybe we're not on the same level anymore, and that's okay. It doesn't mean I'm better than you. It only means I'm different.

Not changing is a detriment. What if we are supposed to spur positive change in everyone else? What if we are supposed to push everyone else out of their boxes?

Instead of getting upset when people say that we've changed, we should simply say, "Thank you for noticing. I've been working hard at being better." Because to change is to be human. To change is to adapt to challenges we've faced. It means we are adjusting to what life has thrown us and doing things differently. If the change they see is us being more cruel, hateful, and thoughtless, then maybe we can say, "Hmmm . . . I should adjust." Otherwise, NAH.

They see that you are not exactly like you used to be, but why is that an insult? Why would you want to be exactly who you used to be? That means you aren't doing your job as a person. It means you're not doing what's necessary. Change is necessary. To be the same person you were last year or last decade means you've learned nothing new and you're doing things the same way and at the same level you used to. It means that you're not growing, and what's not growing is dying. To be the same person you used to be means you're not getting new tools to handle what life throws at you. It means you're insisting on talking the same way, thinking the same way. It means you're not pushing back on what you think is true. Things are constantly changing around you, so why would you stay the same?

I can't stop growing just because it would make somebody more comfortable. My job in the world is not to make other people comfortable. And if they somehow take my evolution, my adjustments, my choices as an affront to their lack of evolution, then I guess I am doing it right. We should all want to change. We should all want to be better. We should all feel like we're more prepared to handle some of the curveballs that are thrown our way. And to be quite honest, a lot of times the things that we have to do, the people we have to be, the places that we have to go will require us to change. We can't be sorry about it.

Your change and your choices aren't about anyone else. They are about you. What is best for you might offend other people because once you start making choices that are truly yours, others might project their failure to do the same on you and resent you for it. That is not your fault, nor is it your business. Grow anyway. Do what's hard anyway. Change anyway.

Imagine this: You and another person both start on the first floor in a climb to the top. You are taking big steps and quickly find yourself on the seventh floor. But when you look down, the other person is only on floor three. Sure, it might make you wanna compare yourself because you started at the same place. The distance is more clear. The thing is, though, we don't go up the stairs at the same pace. Our journeys are different. The dragons we each have to slay are different. Instead of comparing, our job should be to cheer each other on and tell each other to keep going. Maybe we even warn them of the dragons that await and share how we beat ours. But instead we take other people's growth as an affront.

When someone calls you "funny acting," it might mean they

aren't used to the new you, whatever they perceive that to be. You're someone who is known to be quiet, and now you've been using your voice more? Funny acting. You used to allow your friends to make jokes about you, and now you've started telling them they're being rude AF? Funny acting. You used to constantly be the organizer of events, parties, and friend get-togethers, but you stopped because you need to focus more on your grades and extracurriculars? Funny acting.

You know what I say? BE FUNNY ACTING, THEN! If me looking like I'm trying to get my life together is me being funny acting, then call me a clown if you want!

People might think you've changed because they would change if they were in your position. But what's actually changed is their behavior toward you. Often, it is completely outside us. It happens.

What people see as you changing is really you doing what is necessary to meet your goals. It is you doing what is needed to honor your own boundaries. It is actually you trying to ensure that you aren't placing everyone's needs over your own like you used to.

As you evolve, you should not let people weaponize the old you against the new you. There are those who will hate your growth so much that they will remind you of your past in an attempt to piss on your future.

When people want to judge you from four versions of you ago, there's not much you can do. You just gotta keep being this version and accept that they never received the software update cuz their device can't handle the tech upgrade (iPhone 2S faces). You can't come and break your neck trying to get people to see you now when they don't want to.

I'm telling you, people will try it. "Remember when you used to . . . ?"

"Sis, remember when you used to say 'on fleek' unironically? Whew, that was rough for you. But look at you now! You changed! Why can't I change?"

Every auntie in life is good for this, BTW. "OMG, I remember when you used to pee in the bed." Ma'am, that was literally thirty years ago, and I was four. Can you not? (I know I'm an auntie, but I'm gonna try not to be THAT auntie.)

When people remind you of your past selves, tell them yes, you remember them and you're glad they existed, because who you are now is so much better and you're thankful for it. Tell them how proud you are that you, with all your flaws, keep doing the work to make sure you are never that person again. Then smile widely and tell them you wish they'd grow up too. (Okay, maybe don't add that part. I'm still petty. I ain't grown out of that yet.)

We fear change and then attach the guilt of what we could lose to it, further making it harder to welcome it with open arms. I want us to give ourselves permission to grow and change, without guilt.

When my first book came out and instantly hit the *New York Times* bestseller list, my life changed immediately. I went from being a girl who blogs to being an author in an elite club. I was already traveling a lot, but my inquiries tripled, and my fees doubled. I basically lived on planes in between speaking engagements.

What that meant was I stopped being able to write three times a week like I had been doing. As the side-eye sorceress of pop culture happenings, reacting to what was happening in the world with my commentary was what had built my career, and suddenly I didn't have time for it. Why? Because I barely knew what city I was in at any moment from the rapid pace I was on. And I carried a lot of guilt about it. As my audience said "Oooh, I wonder what Luvvie will say about this," on news that was happening, I'd be running (late) to catch another flight, and I'd feel these pangs of fault, not being able to do my job.

What I didn't realize was my job had changed, and that was okay. My job was no longer to be the person sitting at home all the time in her pajamas, reacting to the news of the day. My job now was to take stages, telling people about my lessons, my mistakes, and my triumphs. My job was to make sure the book I had written, a manifesto of my thoughts about life, had the furthest reach it could have. My job was to ensure that a Black woman like me could also get these doors opened for her.

It was change I didn't readily accept, because I was stuck in a cycle of guilt and fear that my audience would think I'd left them behind. That thing that got me to where I was? Turns out it needed to be left behind to get me to where I needed to go.

What I didn't realize is that the people who were upset that I'd "changed" and didn't blog anymore weren't the people I should have been speaking to. The ones who saw my posts on social media and cheered these new adventures on were the ones who mattered. The ones who said "I miss your blog posts, but I LOVE this new season in your life" were the ones who fed my spirit.

I was no longer the girl with the blog updating every day. I had evolved into the bestselling author, the international keynote speaker, the CEO of a media company. I had grown, and that was exactly what I needed, because it allowed my work to have more impact. It also ushered in more attention and scrutiny on my words, and even though that sometimes led to egg on my face, it also led me to being so much more thoughtful than I was before.

What happens when we're given permission early enough to change, to grow? When we are told, "Listen, I already know you're going to have to be different from who you are today, and that's okay. Don't feel guilty about it." How much does that free us, when we know that this isn't something to run away from, but to look forward to? When the people in our lives can say, "I know you have a book tour coming and you'll be MIA. I'll be here when you get back. Because the new life that you're leading is calling for you to be gone more often and I support you"? Whewww! The freedom.

Imagine waking up in the morning and not feeling shame because your friend knows change looks like us not having the same time we used to have on the phone together, or it means we might have to schedule the next time we see each other. Imagine not being worried about who we are offending with the change that is required of us. It gives us wings. We can now do the best work of our lives. We can be the best people possible without constantly being afraid of what we're leaving behind, who we're leaving behind, or who's feeling small as we're trying to be big. When the changes that I need to make aren't met with eye rolls of inconvenience but are met with affirmations of understanding, I have the room to stretch as I need.

We have to learn how to change and how to grow without guilt. Once we do that, we'll be freer in general for it because the fear of change will start to go away a little bit. We begin to learn it's a part of life and something we have to do. We know it might be uncomfortable, but we realize the most uncomfortable things are usually the most necessary things. It can be good to be in our comfort zones, but sometimes the comfort zones insulate us and keep us from doing what we're actually supposed to do.

Give yourself permission to grow wildly. To transform. To change your opinions. To change your surroundings. To change three times a day while on vacation because you've had all these outfits just waiting to see the sun. You ALWAYS have a right to be different from how or who you were, if that is what is in your heart. You have a right to change your mind about your beliefs. You have a right to change political parties after learning more. You have a right to change your profile picture for the fourth time this week.

Change: It's not optional. It's life's necessary and perpetual go-to that can break our hearts, make us scream, thrill us. It will challenge us and sometimes make us wonder if we can make it past the pains of it all. I think about young Fúnmiláyọ̀ and how many times life stretched her till she almost snapped. I wonder how she made it through constant change, and how many times she was afraid of taking the road less traveled but did it anyway. I think about one of her favorite scriptures, Psalm 61: "When my heart is overwhelmed: lead me to the rock that is higher than I." That is what I chant to myself in the times I'm called to grow beyond what feels feasible. I always end up on those high rocks, and I'm thankful.

12

TAKE NO SH*T

We fear ruffling feathers.

 We are afraid of being shunned in any way by the people around us, and we fear coming across as difficult, because at our core, we want community. We want to be liked and we want people to think we are nice. Whether we're kids or full grown, acceptance by other humans is a real need, because it is how we are hardwired. So we try our best to do what others will consider pleasant.

As a result, we swallow our words and our feelings down while plastering a smile on our face, even when we want to scream. We yield to people and then spend our lives being constantly devalued and disrespected. In our need for acceptance, forced niceness ends up doing us a major disservice, as we prioritize others' wants above ours.

When I wrote *I'm Judging You*, some people said, "You wrote a book admitting that you're judging people?" And I said, "Yes, because I am." We're all actually judging each other. The problem is we're judging each other on the things that make no sense: what we look like, who we love, the religion we practice, the color of our skin, our gender.

Instead, we should be judging on other things: Are we showing up in the world in the best way possible? Are we being kind? Are we making sure that we're holding ourselves accountable for other people too? When I say I'm judging you, I'm not judging you because of what you look like; I'm judging you by who you actually are.

I think that we are often wasting our time trying to be nice. Why? Because humans are fickle beings. People are consistently inconsistent about what they want, so when we base our actions on the end goal, which is to be considered nice or anything else, it can be for naught. There is no way you can guarantee that somebody will like you. In the words of Elyana Rausa, "You are not required to set yourself on fire to keep other people warm." So what's the point of trying so hard?

When we go out of our way to people-please, we are placing our value on being as agreeable as we can be in order to be loved or accepted. It is often self-betrayal.

There is nothing wrong with wanting to be "nice," but I don't think that should be our goal. Granted, I'm not saying walk around with the intent of being an asshole. Nah. But being seen as cordial should not be the main motivator of our behavior.

Instead, I think we should aspire to be kind. To be kind is to be generous, fair, honest, helpful, altruistic, gracious, tolerant, understanding, humble, giving, vulnerable, service driven. To be nice is to smile a lot and be chatty with random strangers. Nice is talking about the weather. Kind is caring about whether someone has an umbrella in case it rains.

People have niceness and kindness mixed up. Niceness might mean saying positive things. But kindness is doing positive things: being thoughtful and considerate, prioritizing people's humanity over everything else.

I don't exist in this world for someone to describe me only as "nice" when I'm not in the room. Nice can be empty and shallow and passive. Nice tells me nothing about someone when that is the only thing that is used to describe them. If I ask someone about you and their strongest statement is "She's nice," then I'll assume you're a walking doormat. Or you're someone who is always smiling, even in the moments of strife, which feels dishonest. It says to me that I might need to question you more on how you're really feeling. It tells me nothing of note. Nice is the saltine cracker of adjectives; it's bland.

When we're always trying to be nice, we catch a lot of flak and deal with a lot of people's awful behavior, and we don't hold them accountable. We end up being at the other end of unjust things more than we should, because in our politeness, we relegate our own feelings to the bottom of the barrel.

We don't have to do any of that to be loved. We don't have to bend ourselves backward to have the people who matter see us and cherish us. Even if you're cantankerous, you can still find folks who will stan you!

Mama Fáloyin was one of the kindest people I've ever met. She was also super feisty and took no shit, and people knew that. If anyone tried her, she'd get all Queen Bee on them and sting. But her heart was huge, and to her, everyone was a neighbor she was responsible for. If people were in a bind, they'd knock on her door, and she would listen to them, help if she could, and send them off with a Tupperware of food and a truly meant prayer of "God bless you, ọmọ mi" (my child).

When she died, she died loved by droves of people. There were all sorts of dignitaries and people who had known her closely for decades paying their respects. Granny was Team No Chill, and she was adored. She wasn't a woman who felt the need to placate others if that wasn't her real thought in the moment.

Some of the stories I've heard about her are legendary, especially from when she was younger, before I was even born. When my mom was in elementary school, her teacher took some scissors to her hair as punishment for her not having her homework done. My grandma flipped out! The next day, she took my mom to school herself, while holding scissors. She got there and asked for the teacher. Why was Grandma there with scissors? Because she said since the lady cut her child's hair, she was there to cut the teacher's hair too. She was dead-ass serious. It took ten people kneeling down in front of Grandma, begging her and invoking God's mercy, for her to abandon the mission and go back home. That teacher never tried anything else with any of the Fáloyin kids again.

My grandma could have let it slide, but you know what would have happened if she had? The teacher would have thought it was okay to keep doing extreme things like that. This is why I push back against the constant encouragement to take the high road when we are harmed. I think some high roads need to stay under construction.

Let's talk about taking the high road, because it is definitely a thing people tell us we should do to somehow be the better person. You know the one time I disagreed with my fave Michelle Obama was when she said, "When they go low, we go high." Honestly, when people go low, sometimes we have to meet them there. If you go low, I might go gutter.

I am not a fan of asking folks to turn the other cheek in situations where they shouldn't feel obligated to do so. On certain occasions, the insistence on taking the high road is actually harming us more than it's helping. Putting harmony over justice and civility over amends is a harmful practice if we are telling people to constantly bypass defending themselves or standing against what is awry. I'm not for the kumbaya of it all. People read that Jesus told us to turn the other cheek and love our neighbors, but that is the SAME person who also flipped tables in a temple when folks did too much.

You don't owe your bully niceness. You don't owe someone who tries to abuse you "the higher road." And you surely do not owe someone who is mean to you politeness.

The need for niceness permeates how we move through the world, address those in our daily lives, and even combat systems that don't serve us. We are always trying to be "civil" above all else, and I think it is part of why the world is a dumpster fire.

In June 2018, America's forty-fifth president (and the first walking Cheeto in the White House) signed an executive order that led to the separation of migrant children and their parents at the United States border. The people's champ and forever truthteller, Maxine Waters, was very vocal in her rightful critique about it, saying: "We don't know what damage has been done to these children. All that we know is they're in cages. They're in prisons. They're in jails. I don't care what they call it, that's where they are and Mr. President, we will see you every day, every hour of the day, everywhere that we are to let you know you cannot get away with this."*

NO LIES TOLD. The next day, her own party called her comments "divisive." If the truth is divisive, then what it's pointing out must be especially repugnant. Chuck Schumer said, "We all have to remember to treat our fellow Americans, all of our fellow Americans, with the kind of civility and respect we expect will be afforded to us." Sir, those kids in cages aren't being treated with ANY type of civility, so please have a damb seat.

When will people realize that niceness and taking the high road are not going to save us? You don't make change by being civil to the people who are not looking at other people as full humans. There's a thin line between being nice and enabling trash.

If we can't put justice over niceness, what are we doing as a people? Where are we going to end up if we continue to turn the other cheek when somebody harms us? The people who harm us are not being told to be civil or nice or to take the high road. It's always the person who's been victimized in some way who is told to make that choice. Does that serve us? We're going to be civil and we're going to nice our way into bondage.

Here's the thing about villains and other people who harm us.

*Jamie Ehrlich, "Maxine Waters Encourages Supporters to Harass Trump Administration Officials," CNN, June 25, 2018, https://www.cnn.com/2018/06/25/politics/maxine-waters-trump-officials/index.html.

Usually when somebody does something to you that is not just disrespectful but harmful to you as a person, you're already past the point of civility. This person isn't looking at you as a full human being. You can't change their behavior or affect the outcome by being really nice about it. This is why people who insist on politeness miss the point. All this "We should be nicer" gets us nowhere, because if people wanna take offense to our words, they will find a reason. Nah, I'm not nice. Yes, I will challenge your nonsense.

Why do people prioritize civility over justice? Justice does not come just because you're begging for it. Justice does not come because you're being nice about the other person who's not giving you justice. So I don't understand the insistence on this high road.

When you're in a fight for your life, when you're in a fight for the world, when you're in a fight against something like white supremacy, how sweet your tone is won't be a factor in getting basic rights. You don't civil your way to justice.

And when we talk about folks protesting in the streets, people get mad because "Well, it's not orderly how people protest." When half of the country is wishing for immigrants to be separated from their family members and we're being told to be civil about it, what is civility doing for us? What is this niceness doing? We're prioritizing the wrong thing.

Someone (some thing, some system, some power structure) convinced us that if we were more civil or respectable or dressed nicer, we'd be more worthy of justice or love or other good things.

We are worthy of all those things TODAY. Now. Even if we cuss and swear and we don't form our sentences perfectly. Even if we aren't buttoned up. Even if we mess up sometimes.

I want us to push past the idea that civility or niceness is the key. I'm not saying we have to be douchebags to everybody. I'm not saying we have to walk around being angry. I'm saying that when it's time for us to challenge systems and people, how we say it should not nullify the message. We can still be kind, but we do not have to be nice. And our needs and wants are valid even if we don't express them neatly.

We need to TAKE NO SHIT, and if you need permission to do that, consider this that.

This doesn't mean you address everyone who brings trash to you or says something about you. You don't have that kind of time. It also doesn't mean you accept every invitation to fight. Nah. It means in the times when it's called for—and you will know those times—do not feel bad for meeting someone in the basement. This doesn't mean you're a bad person or you're immature. It means you made a decision to engage with someone as they asked for it. Sometimes you gotta remind people that messing with you comes with a cost. It be like that, and folks gotta deal. And sometimes, taking no shit might even look like silence to the person who is trying to force you to pay attention to them.

We've spent so much time telling people to be nice and civil that we feel like we have no room to defend ourselves in a world that's constantly at war with us. You don't owe anyone civility if they have traumatized you. Nor do you owe them a hello, even in person. They can take this full side-eye.

I am calling on us to challenge ourselves to be more truthful, to be more outspoken. Be kinder, speak louder. Use your voice and don't let people silence you or make you feel bad because they don't see what you're doing as civil or nice. Fight for people who are not you. Insist on being uncomfortable and taking yourself outside your usual space to fight for other people who might not have the right to fight, or the voice, or the money, or the stature, or the positioning. That's kindness.

I aspire to be kind, and I hope my actions are kind. I hope when I'm gone, someone somewhere describes me as such, because my life is a journey in giving as much as I've received. Kind is compassionate. And we can be kind and generous, but we need to take no shit. The first person we need to be kind to is ourselves.

Grandma was Team Take No Shit. When she was younger, there was a time when she was taking a seminar at her church to go up in the ranks. She was the first woman allowed to even take it, so it was a big deal! When she completed all the requirements for it and called the church to say she was coming for her plaque, the pastor said he wasn't going to give it to her. The moment Grandma heard that, she hulked up, put on some pants, and rode to that church. See, Mama Fáloyin didn't wear pants often. She was usually in a dress or caftan. She only wore pants for two reasons: Because she was cold. Or because she needed to fight.

Well, when she showed up at the church in her fighting pants, the pastor didn't want the smoke, so he went into his office and locked the door. Who born him to say NO to her getting what she had earned?

What did Mama Fáloyin do? She stood in front of his office door and refused to leave. "You can be in there all day, but I'll be out here waiting. I'm not going anywhere until you give me my certificate."

My grandfather, who was usually the peacekeeper, backed her up and said, "You better give it to her. She will be here all day, and I will be right here behind her." I STAN a supportive bae! Long story short, she walked out of that church with what she came for. The pastor, who wasn't used to any of that, learned on that day that Fúnmiláyọ̀ Ọmọ Láṣọ́rè is not one to trifle with.

They cherished her at that church. If she was missing from church for too many weeks in a row, they'd send a contingent to go visit her to see if she was doing okay or check on whether they'd somehow offended her. But really, they loved her dearly.

When my grandmother died in 2011 in Nigeria, the high-ranking women in her church insisted on being the ones to dress her instead of the morticians. They wanted her to have the utmost care as she was prepared. They wanted to send her off with love.

We traveled to Nigeria as a family to give her a proper send-off. I was in the room as Mama Fáloyin got her last bath. I remember trying to take in everything that was happening, because I didn't wanna miss anything about it. I was acutely aware of the fact that I was bearing witness to a sacred space and ritual. Even as the chemicals in the room made it hard to breathe, I dared not move. The tears that streamed down my face weren't just from the formaldehyde—they were also my grief and gratitude.

I remember staring at the body of the person who was the prototype of womanhood for me. As they dressed her, they prayed over her. It was done with such care too, putting her in one of the white gowns she wore for church that my aunt had picked out. They draped one of her favorite purple sashes over her with sanctity. My heart throbbed because it was the utmost display of love. My goodness. To be cherished and respected like that, having lived openly, freely, totally. I was affirmed by it because it was the pinnacle of a life well lived.

She did it on her own terms, even when she was painted into corners. She did it joyfully and genuinely, fiery and full of moxie.

A life well lived is not one where you made sure the rooms you were in didn't have friction. A life well lived isn't about plastering a fake smile on your face. A life well lived is not about how many people you did not upset. A life well lived is one where you commit to being kind. Where you connect your humanity to that of others, and it shows in the way you move through the world. And that's what we gotta do.

We will ruffle feathers. We might be the villains in a few people's stories. We might even blow up a few bridges. But our worth is not based on how much we acquiesced to the people we knew. The goal is to betray ourselves less.

So, be kind, but take no shit.

13

FIGHT FEAR

We fear fear.

 Fear is a hater. Fear will have you sitting down when you should be standing up. Fear will have you not saying that thing that is necessary when you need to. Fear will talk you out of your purpose so quick that your destiny gets whiplash.

Fear is real, primitive, and innate. It's one of the most natural emotions. To not have any fear is actually a physiological disorder called Urbach-Wiethe disease, and it happens when the brain's amygdala is damaged. True story.

We are not supposed to be walking around fearlessly. Our angst is a biological necessity because it keeps us safe from doing dumbass things without safety nets.

To be afraid is to be human. But I think that's assuring: it's really cool to know that we're all out here walking around with varying levels of "WTF is this?" happening at any given time. Some of us have learned to hide it better or handle it so it doesn't overtake us. Some people make choices to move past their doubts, knowing it might not work out, but they will try anyway, while others can point to pivotal moments when they have let fear be their main decision factor. But we all feel it.

I want to always be the type of person who overcomes her doubts. But in my life, I have been the type of person who let fear dictate her decisions more times than I can count. My journey to where I am today was longer than it could have been because I let fear stop me from owning my purpose and my passion and my profession for a long time. And it wasn't until I made the decision to push past those scary moments that I started seeing my life move forward in ways that blew my mind.

I wrote this book because I remember being young and feeling alone in my anxieties about everyday life. No one ever told me it was okay to be afraid, and that what I needed to do was move forward anyway. I tried to figure so much of life out on my own. I wanted YOU to have this book so you wouldn't have to feel so alone or weird for simply feeling scared of so much in a world that can feel like a tangled forest.

Choosing to fight fear is not like joining some lifelong club that once you're in, you can't get out. Nah. It's a moment-by-moment, day-by-day decision. The biggest scaredy-cat in the world can decide to do something brave at any moment. It might be as small as ordering a doughnut they've never had. Or as big as proposing to the love of their life. Or as audacious as going skydiving because their friend asked them.

We are all fighting battles with the world, systems, ourselves. Battles that are easy to lose. It's so much easier to keep doing what feels comfortable. What feels safe. But then we might look up one day and realize that we've safety-netted ourselves into lives that feel like cages. Cages can get comfortable, but comfort is overrated. Being quiet is comfortable. Keeping things the way they've been is comfortable. But all comfort does is maintain the status quo.

What forces us to live comfortable lives that might not serve us?

What forces the people in our lives to shrink? It is partly caused by our fears and other people's angst layered on top of each other.

Do we realize how often we pass on our fears to other people? Do we realize how much we impose the things we are afraid of on the people we love and care about every single day? I know exactly why people are afraid of choosing the path that is unfamiliar, of experiencing things and being free. We are constantly telling people to be scared.

I took a trip to Mexico one year and posted on social media, casually, about loving how I was getting the opportunity to eat mangoes every single day because they are my favorite fruit. I got so many comments from people who were warning me that I would end up on the toilet throne, because when they ate mangoes, they had the runs. Meanwhile, it was day six and I was perfectly okay, and continued to be. The same thing happened when, before the trip, I told people I was going to another country and was told to "watch out for kidnappers." Or when I said I was sitting outside and someone warned me about how the mosquitoes were going to make a meal out of me. Mind you, at no point was I asking people for advice. I was simply sharing what I was doing, and I was instantly met with tales of misfortune.

I get it. The world is scary. Shit happens. But we lead our lives with so much fear. We're so busy constantly bracing for impact that we stay right where we are, too afraid to move, because that monster we think is around the corner will jump out.

Sometimes this anxiety comes from our loved ones. The generational curses we talk about breaking can be limitations that those we love have habitually placed on us. The weapons that have formed might actually be from our families and friends, who meant well but ended up using ammunition of apprehension on us. Breaking cycles can mean unlearning what those closest to us have taught us.

How free would we be if we weren't being tethered down by other people's anxieties, doubts, and insecurities? How high could we fly if people weren't pulling at our ankles to keep us grounded to earth because that's where they are? How loud would we be if we weren't afraid of people calling us intimidating for our assurance?

You deserve to be free of other people's weight. You deserve to be unbuckled from other people's doubts. You carry enough of your own. We all deserve to walk light.

When people try to drop their bags of fears at our feet, let us drop-kick the bag back to them. We don't want it. I'm not holding your doubts. I'm not making space in MY life for YOUR angst. I will not sleep under a blanket of your dread. It's not mine to carry. No thank you.

Sure, we can live lives where we are minimally afraid because we've covered ourselves in bubble wrap and don't take any risks, but THAT life is boring. That life is wasted. That life is a version of fluorescent beige. Your gravestone will be all, "They were here." Dassit. Dassall. You'll get to heaven and God will roll His/Her/Their eyes at you. All this breath, all this movement, all this BE-ING. And you wasted it being the person version of a flavorless rice cake. What will you have done that you were proud of?

When I'm dead and gone, I want to have left a mark. It's like in the movie *Coco*: we only truly die when our names no longer pass off someone's tongue. I want to be missed. I want my absence felt. I want my contributions to be bigger than my small stature. I want this world to be better because I was here. And if I'm moving with fear and doubt and anxiety first, I'm standing in no gaps, writing in fluff, speaking in whispers.

I am not fearless. But I've learned to start pushing past fear because oftentimes, the fear itself is scarier than whatever is on the other side. It's like being afraid to walk through a dark hallway. If you close your eyes and run through it, you'll be okay. And you'll look back and say, "That wasn't that bad."

For me, fighting fear is facing freedom. We owe it to ourselves and we owe it to the people who see us, or surround us, or love us.

We owe it to ourselves to lighten our load and drop dead weight. Drop it all. The friends who don't really have your back. The partner who makes you feel worthless. The trauma that makes you self-sabotage. The self-doubt that makes you think you're not good enough.

We owe it to ourselves to climb the mountains that feel too tall.

The world isn't going to get less scary. I'm basically lowering my expectations on that. But we need to get braver by committing to not letting the hard things stop us. We must keep doing the things that scare us, knowing that what is right is often the opposite of what is easy.

Get on with it, and start by forgiving yourself for not having had the courage to do something you wish you did in the past.

Forgive yourself for not speaking up in moments that might have called for it. Forgive yourself for the mistakes you've made that now feel avoidable. You did your best with the information you had and understood at the time.

Everyone who has done major things has started with one step. Most people who did major things or changed the world got the idea and one day decided to take one step, followed by another, followed by another. Rome wasn't built in a day, but the bricks they laid to build it had to begin on some day.

Those dreams we have the audacity to dream? They can't stay on the "wish list" pile forever. Well, they can, but then what was the point? We actually have to DO.

So, in case you need encouragement to BE, SAY, DO, here it is, because really cool things can be waiting for you on the other side of fear. You have a long, beautiful life ahead of you, and this is what I didn't know I needed to hear at your age. The big things we are so afraid of doing because they seem too ginormous for us, we must do. Even if we do them poorly. Ask that scary question. Write that book. Learn that language. Check off the bucket list. Apply to that number-one-ranked college program. Run for that school office. Try out for the varsity team. Purge your shoe closet (*looks at self*). Run that marathon. (This is not my ministry, and I still think marathons are conspiracies. Of who? I'm not sure.) Go on that audition. Make that move!

Do all of that. Or do none of that, if that's what you're compelled to do. But that thing that you keep thinking about, but you keep stopping because you're afraid? DO THAT THING.

In the moments when I want to run back to what's comfortable or I dare to cower in the face of doubt, I think about Olúfúnmiláyọ̀ Juliana Fáloyin, my guardian angel and my prototype of a professional troublemaker. That God-loving, favor-finding, whole-face-smiling unicorn of a woman. I think about her starting her life from scratch by herself at the age of eighteen. I reflect on the woman who doctors told wouldn't speak again when she had a stroke. I can't help but muse on my muse who moved through the world boldly confident that God and her faith were bigger than any fear.

I carry and will continue to carry my grandmother with me everywhere I go. Every day, I look down at my right hand, at the gold filigree ring I never take off. It's the one Grandma gave me one day when I saw her wearing it and instantly squealed how much I loved it. Without hesitation, she took the ring off and handed it to me. It's funny that it adorns the middle finger of my dominant hand. It works.

A professional troublemaker is someone who is committed to being authentically themselves while speaking the truth and doing some scary shit. Here is to us, daring to live boldly. I owe it to Mama Fáloyin, my favorite troublemaker, to do this. When fear tries to stop me, I need to put on my pants, say a little prayer of strength, and dance for twenty minutes to celebrate my insistence on conquering doubt.

Fear is a hater, a liar, and a cheat. To be FEARLESS is to commit to not doing LESS because of our fears. We owe ourselves fearlessness, and we can start now.

Acknowledgments

First of all, thank YOU, RISING TROUBLEMAKER, for taking the time with my work. To have people find value in my work is such an honor. For that, lemme bless you with some prayers. May you never stub your toe on the side of the bed in the middle of the night. May you always season your food perfectly. May your pot of rice be perfectly cooked always. Amen.

Shout-out to meeee, cuz I DID THAT! Sometimes stopping to smell the roses looks like high-fiving yourself, and this book is something that feels revel-worthy. Also, people write books and forget how to act. I am people.

My life truly is a testimony of God's grace, and this is yet another thing I've done that I hope makes Her/Him/Them proud. I am constantly shown that my steps are ordered by forces greater than me, and for that I am thankful.

Grandma, I know you're still working on my behalf and fighting for me from Beyond. Thank you. I hope you love this.

It took a village for this book to come together. Thanks to my agent, Kristyn Keene Benton, whose belief in my work pushes me forward. She also didn't side-eye me anytime I called her with some random idea.

Thanks to the team at Penguin Random House and Philomel Books for believing in this book, this message, and my voice! Props to Jill Santopolo, my editor, who championed this book!

To the man I married, Carnell: thank you for playing many roles, as best friend, husband, and anchor. You see me in ways I'm sometimes not audacious enough to see myself. You don't let me have limits because you see stardust all over me. I remember when I finished this book and said, "Wow. This is the best thing I've ever written." You replied with, "I'm so proud of you, and it should be. You're the best YOU you've ever been." And my heart grinned like a Cheshire cat because words of affirmation are my top love language, and you get me. And I thanked God, once again, for blessing me with a life partner who affirms my very being. Mr. Jones, you're dope AF.

I am surrounded by love and people who prove that there is GREATNESS in the world, in the form of soft places to land.

Shout-out to my family. I thank God for my mom. I am the daughter of Oluyemisi, who is the daughter of Fúnmiláyọ̀, who is the daughter of Celina. From her, I've learned generosity and the art of stunting when it is necessary. She is love in walking form.

I gotta shout-out my big sister, Kofo. You are the cheerleader of life, gist partner, dance partner, matron of honor, sometimes twin. Your heart is gold, and you deserve all the good things life has to offer. Thanks for the grandma stories I forgot too. Whew, we got some of our funny from that lady.

So many thank-yous to my aunt, Bunmi B. She's the one I called over and over again to tell me more stories of Grandma and verify my facts, and she provided the oríkì. She's a quiet storm, a woman of integrity, and a joy bringer. Thank you for always picking up my calls, for being the family historian, and for that laugh that brightens up a room.

Our family is a true tribe unto itself: Bimbola, Morayo, Dele, Rolake, Wonuola, Folarin. I'd fight for y'all, but you already know this.

I am inspired by my nieces and nephews, who I also wrote this book for: Dejah, Destiny, Tooni, Obafemi, Darius, Kami, David. Hoping to win the Dope Aunt Award for having your names in this book. I'm so proud of who you are all growing up to be and honored to be your soft place to land.

LOVE to my FRAMILY (friends who become family) for peer-pressuring me into greatness and being everlasting dream-enablers.

They're the ones I call when something feels BIG, almost too big, and they always remind me that "If not you, then who?" They push me onward and upward, constantly loaning me power whenever I'm lacking. Thank you, and I love y'all!!!

Shout-out to my mentors, who continue to speak my name in rooms and who are constantly co-conspiring with me to see my dreams come true: Thasunda Brown Duckett, Lisa Stone, Jana Rich, Sandra Williams, Richelle Parham. And SO MANY MORE. I am surrounded by women who embolden my life.

ALL THE LOVE to the citizens of LuvvNation, the most thoughtful, funny, chill-deficient play cousins on the interwebs. Building a safe space in a dumpster-fire world is one of the best things I could have done, and when people tell me my audience is amazing, I grin. Why? Because if they're a reflection of me, then they are proof that there is ample goodness in this world. LuvvCousins are the best!

This section could be a tome in itself, and there are so many more people who are significant to me who are not named here. You are probably one. But for real, thank you to everyone who sees, reads, buys, shares, and takes in my work.

Thank YOU for seeing me.

Luvvie